HASHEM IS MY LIGHT

HASHEM IS MY LIGHT

mining le-Dovid (Psalm 27)
for insight and inspiration

Rabbi Elchanan Shoff

KODESH PRESS

This book was originally published under the title *Lord, Get Me High!* and is republished (September 2019) under the title *Hashem is My Light*.

Published & Distributed by
Kodesh Press L.L.C.
New York, NY
kodeshpress@gmail.com

Table of Contents

Dedicated with love to my dear friend

Rabbi Moshe Heideman

Your kindness and support mean almost as much to me as your undying friendship. You are exceptional, and I am lucky to be your friend. Thank you for all that you do for me and for *Klal Yisrael*. The positive and inspirational impact that you have already had, and continue to have on others is nothing short of magnificent.

May you and your wonderful family know nothing but joy, happiness, *nachas*, and success.

Dedicated by the Pollack Families in loving
memory of our granparents

Meir Yoel ben Shlomo

Rachel bas Eliyahu

Herschel Shmuel ben
Menachem Mendel Leib

and

Leah Esther bas Avraham

Psalm 27

1. By David; Hashem is my light and my salvation whom shall I fear? Hashem is my life's strength, whom shall I dread? 2. My tormentors and enemies against me, it is they who stumble and fall. 3. Though an army would besiege me, my heart would not fear; though war would arise against me, in this I trust. 4. I have asked one thing from Hashem, that I sit in the house of Hashem all my life, that I see the pleasantness of Hashem, and that I visit His sanctuary. That He protect me in His canopy on a day of evil, that He conceal me in the privacy of His tent, and that He elevate me to a strong rock. 5. That He conceal me in His *sukkah* on a day of evil, and conceal me in the inside of his tent, He will raise me up on a rock. 6. Now my head is raised above my enemies around me and I will slaughter offerings in his tent accompanied by *teruah* [joyous song]; I will sing and chant praise to Hashem. 7. Hashem, hear my voice when I call out; be gracious to me and answer me. 8. In your behalf, my heart has said, "Seek My Presence." Your presence Hashem do I seek. 9. Do not hide Your presence from me, do not repel Your servant in anger, You were my Helper, do not abandon me, do not forsake me, God of my salvation. 10. When my father and mother abandoned me, Hashem gathered me in. 11. Teach me Your way Hashem, and lead me on the path of integrity because of those who watch me. 12. Do not deliver me up to the will of my foes, for false witnesses have risen up against me and one who sanctimoniously does wrong. 13. Had I not trusted that I would see the goodness of Hashem in the land of life! 14. Hope to Hashem, strengthen yourself and He will give you courage, and hope to Hashem.

תהילים כ"ז

א) לְדָוִד ה' אוֹרִי וְיִשְׁעִי מִמִּי אִירָא ה' מָעוֹז חַיַּי מִמִּי אֶפְחָד : ב) בִּקְרֹב עָלַי מְרֵעִים לֶאֱכֹל אֶת בְּשָׂרִי צָרַי וְאֹיְבַי לִי הֵמָּה כָשְׁלוּ וְנָפָלוּ : ג) אִם תַּחֲנֶה עָלַי מַחֲנֶה לֹא יִירָא לִבִּי אִם תָּקוּם עָלַי מִלְחָמָה בְּזֹאת אֲנִי בוֹטֵחַ : ד) אַחַת שָׁאַלְתִּי מֵאֵת ה' אוֹתָהּ אֲבַקֵּשׁ שִׁבְתִּי בְּבֵית ה' כָּל יְמֵי חַיַּי לַחֲזוֹת בְּנֹעַם ה' וּלְבַקֵּר בְּהֵיכָלוֹ : ה) כִּי יִצְפְּנֵנִי בְּסֻכֹּה בְּיוֹם רָעָה יַסְתִּרֵנִי בְּסֵתֶר אָהֳלוֹ בְּצוּר יְרוֹמְמֵנִי : ו) וְעַתָּה יָרוּם רֹאשִׁי עַל אֹיְבַי סְבִיבוֹתַי וְאֶזְבְּחָה בְאָהֳלוֹ זִבְחֵי תְרוּעָה אָשִׁירָה וַאֲזַמְּרָה לַה' : ז) שְׁמַע ה' קוֹלִי אֶקְרָא וְחָנֵּנִי וַעֲנֵנִי : ח) לְךָ אָמַר לִבִּי בַּקְּשׁוּ פָנָי אֶת פָּנֶיךָ ה' אֲבַקֵּשׁ : ט) אַל תַּסְתֵּר פָּנֶיךָ מִמֶּנִּי אַל תַּט בְּאַף עַבְדֶּךָ עֶזְרָתִי הָיִיתָ אַל תִּטְּשֵׁנִי וְאַל תַּעַזְבֵנִי אֱ-לֹהֵי יִשְׁעִי : י) כִּי אָבִי וְאִמִּי עֲזָבוּנִי וַה' יַאַסְפֵנִי : יא) הוֹרֵנִי ה' דַּרְכֶּךָ וּנְחֵנִי בְּאֹרַח מִישׁוֹר לְמַעַן שׁוֹרְרָי : יב) אַל תִּתְּנֵנִי בְּנֶפֶשׁ צָרָי כִּי קָמוּ בִי עֵדֵי שֶׁקֶר וִיפֵחַ חָמָס : יג) לוּלֵא הֶאֱמַנְתִּי לִרְאוֹת בְּטוּב ה' בְּאֶרֶץ חַיִּים : יד) קַוֵּה אֶל ה' חֲזַק וְיַאֲמֵץ לִבֶּךָ וְקַוֵּה אֶל ה' :

Introduction

It is the custom in Ashkenazic communities to recite *Le-Dovid* (Psalm 27) twice daily, from the beginning of the month of Elul through the conclusion of the holiday season, at Shmini Atzeres.[1] Clearly there must be some reason why we recite this Psalm so often during this season.[2] Rather than offer some sort of a one line answer that one could easily recycle as *dvar Torah* material at the table, this slim volume is an attempt to take a serious look at fourteen different themes, highlighted in the fourteen verses of this powerful chapter of *Tehillim*. It is my sincerest prayer

---

1. *Matteh Ephraim* (581:6), *Shulchan Aruch Ha-Rav* (*Siddur, Hilchos Krias Shema u-Tefillah*), *Kitzur Shulchan Aruch* (128:2), *Mishnah Berurah* (581:2), Rabbi Yosef Eliyahu Henkin's *Shaalos u-Teshuvos Gevuros Eliyahu* (*Orach Chaim* 155:1), and *Luach Eretz Yisrael* (*Rosh Chodesh Elul* of Rav Yechiel Michel Tukachinsky). See also the important work on this subject of Rabbi Eliezer Brodt in his *Likkutei Eliezer* (Jerusalem 2010) Chapter 1 pp. 1-13. See also the excellent article by HaGaon Rabbi Yehuda Spitz, "Of Elul, L'David, and Golems," which can be accessed at http://ohr.edu/4886

2. There is a degree of Divine guidance in the customs that become Jewish practice, see *Teshuvos Maharik* 9:1, 54:1, *Teshuvos Matteh Yosef*, O.C. 2 (Constantinople 1717), and *Pachad Yitzchak* (Lampronti), s.v. *minhag*, p. 137a. See also R. Yisrael of Kozhnitz *Shearis Yisrael*, *Menachem Tzion* (*Nitzavim*) of R. Menachem Mendel of Riminov, and *Taamei ha-Minhagim* 754. See also Aryeh Kaplan's *Handbook of Jewish Thought*, Chapter 13, p. 261.

that by considering in depth some of the magnificent messages of King David, we will all be inspired to be even more effective in our spiritual quests.

"Its measure is longer than the earth, and wider than the sea."[3] One could easily spend a lifetime exploring just one chapter of the Torah. We are just scratching the surface here. Thank you for joining me on this thrilling journey.

3. *Iyov* 11:9.

Acknowledgements

The thrill of studying authentic Torah far surpasses any other experience in my life. To be able to devote myself to spreading the dynamic experience that is engaging with Jewish tradition, keeping the mitzvos with passion, and loving God and mankind is such a great privilege; one that I know that I am not worthy of. I really do appreciate what a gift it is. Thank You, Hashem.

One of the most absolutely mind-boggling phenomena is how interconnected we all are. Sitting here, writing these words on a computer keyboard, while watching them appear on a monitor, with using programs running on operating systems, all the while using electricity, sitting at a desk, wearing clothing, means that likely hundreds of thousands of people were involved for me to do my simple task. People opened their stores, arrived to work at the power plant, designed, fashioned and delivered the buttons to the people who then attached them to a shirt whose process was equally complex. It ought to give us pause, when we consider even the simplest of things, like fresh daily bread and milk, and how many people are involved in some way in bringing those items from the earliest stages of planting to the Google Shopping Express worker who leaves them for us at our door. And so acknowledgements are crucial. Because we can do nothing alone. Animals are born and can quickly fend for themselves—but humans need years of careful tending to before we are capable of surviving. If we spent our lives doing nothing but thanking everyone who has contributed fairly directly to our wellbeing, we'd never finish. I owe so much to my parents, and my in-laws, our heroes. They are models of what it means to live selflessly, and for others in the most inspiring of ways. My siblings and brothers- and sisters-in-law are nothing short of remarkable. The knowledge that we are part of a solid loving committed group of Torah families seeking earnestly to lead lives of meaning and Torah values imbues us with great optimism hope and courage, that we'd surely have no ability to access otherwise. I am blessed to have had wonderful Rabbeim, to have studied in Yeshivas that understood me and cared about me enough to help me change behaviors and channel character traits effectively. It is a great honor to serve as Rabbi of the Beis Knesses at Faircrest Heights, in Los Angeles. Our small, new, growing community is brimming with optimism, excitement, happiness, and positive Jewish experiences. May we be blessed to watch it grow and impact the community beyond our wildest dreams. My children give me unending joy. I do not take them for granted. Thank you, Hashem, for Shifra, Esther Faiga, Yocheved, and Yaakov Chaim. Please give us the merit to raise them *le-Torah, le-chuppah, u-le-maasim tovim.* I am grateful to my wife, Sara, for being devoted to our family, and to our community. Whatever I have, and whatever I can teach or give you, is hers.

This book exists because many people stepped forward to help. Thank you for believing in me. Not everybody is mentioned in the dedication pages. I owe special thanks to Tanya Freeman, for her commitment to making this Torah available. May Hashem reward you beyond your wildest dreams for your constant selflessness and kindness. Sara Rosenbaum is the best editor ever. Thanks Sara—I really appreciate your work! Thank you as well to Rabbi Alec Goldstein of Kodesh Press. You have been wonderful, quick and efficient, accessible, and true to your word. It has been amazing working with you, and I anticipate that someone of your integrity and drive will see great success in all areas! Lastly, thank you, dear reader, for picking this up. I hope that this will make some small contribution to your learning and your life.

Elchanan Shoff

Los Angeles, 5775

1

Don't Bark like a Dog!

לְדָוִד ה׳ אוֹרִי וְיִשְׁעִי מִמִּי אִירָא ה׳ מָעוֹז חַיַּי מִמִּי אֶפְחָד :

By David; Hashem is my light and my salvation whom shall I
fear? Hashem is my life's strength, whom shall I dread?

Light and Salvation

This verse tells us about Rosh Hashanah and Yom Kippur, teaches
the Midrash.[1] Hashem is our light (*ori*) on Rosh Hashanah, and
our salvation (*yishi*) on Yom Kippur. In fact, the combined
gematria (numerical value) of *zikaron* and *kippurim*—the proper
names of Rosh Hashanah and Yom Kippur, respectively—add
up to 639, the same value as the words, *Hashem ori ve-yishi.*[2]

---

1. *Vayikra Rabbah* 21:4. See also *Shem Tov Katan* cited in *Siddur Ha-
Ari Maharash* regarding the 13 times that Hashem's name is mentioned
herein, and why it must therefore be recited during this time of year,
when the 13 *middos* of Hashem shine.
2. *Panim Yafos, Acharei Mos* 16:29, s.v. *ve-keivan*, p. 268, Gross ed.

Life for Real Reason

The one and only reason that we ask Hashem to grant us life every Rosh Hashanah and Yom Kippur, explains the *Panim Yafos*,[3] is in order to achieve true service of Hashem, and fulfill His mitzvos. When a person offers his existence as a vehicle completely altruistically motivated to serving Hashem and working for Him, then he is granted life. *Zachrenu le-chaim, Melech chafetz ba-chaim, ve-chasvenu be-sefer ha-chaim, le-maancha, Elokim chaim*: "Remember us for life, King Who desires life, and inscribe us in the Book of Life, for Your sake, living God." We do not simply ask for life. We ask for a life that will contribute to the world in only the most positive ways. *Le-maancha Elokim chaim*. If it is not *le-maancha*, "for Your sake," then we must truly be uninterested in a longer life.[4] We would not have the audacity to beg Hashem for life just so that we can find the time to polish off a few more beers.

"Hashem is my life's strength." The *Panim Yafos* explains that this verse expresses the sentiment above. Hashem is my salvation, and light, and He is my life's strength; I have nothing else. For that reason, I do not fear anyone or anything, for I can know that I am living for Hashem. If one is truly devoted to Hashem, and simply wants His will to be performed, fear dissipates. We fear things going poorly because we feel that we know what is best, and yet factors that we cannot control can derail our plans. A person whose entire plan is no more than "whatever Hashem wants" has nothing to fear!

---

3. Ibid., p. 269. See also *Panim Yafos* to *Nitzavim* 30:1.
4. See the important comments of R. Yisrael Salanter cited in *Alei Shur* Vol. 2, p. 419, and *Daas Chochmah u-Musar,* Vol. 2 p. 288 to this effect.

"Master of the world," said Avraham, "if it's clear to you that should I have children, they would disappoint you, then I would prefer to remain childless." And King David said the very same thing.[5]

Don't Act Like a Dog

The Zohar[6] speaks unfavorably about those who enter the Days of Awe and bark like dogs, saying, *"hav hav."* Dogs barking make a sound like *hav hav. Hav* is also the Aramaic word for "give." People can spend their time reciting to Hashem a laundry list of demands: "Give me life, give me wealth, give me insight," and resembling a dog.[7] So, explains the *Panim Yafos*, what we

---

5. *Bereshis Rabbah* 44:9, See also *Ha-Kesav ve-ha-Kabbalah* to *Bereshis* 15:3, s.v. *hen li.*

6. *Tikkunei Zohar* 22a.

7. In *Nedarim* 24a, the Talmud describes the dissatisfied feelings of a person involved in a relationship where he can only take and not give with the words, "I am not a dog, that I only get from you can give nothing." A dog is seen as the ultimate taker in his relationship with a human. The Talmud contrasts this with the perspective of the person who is only giving, and receives nothing, and explains his feelings as, "I am not a king, that you can only take from me, and give me nothing." The polar opposites are kings and dogs. Perhaps this sheds light upon the comments of Avner in *Shmuel* II 3:8-10, after his kindness of so many years was unappreciated by the family of Saul, when he exclaimed, "Am I the chief dog-watcher of Judah? Shall I perform acts of kindness for the house of your father Saul, for his brothers and friends... for just as Hashem has sworn to David, so shall I do for him. To remove the kingship from the house of Saul and to establish the throne of David upon Israel and upon Judah, from Dan to Beersheva!" Once he identified a knack for taking and taking without giving, he realized that this was not place for kingship, which is all about giving, but instead a place of dogs. And so he said, "I am not a dog-watcher," and I know just who is meant to be the king, and now I see that it cannot be someone acting like a dog.

must do is ask for things not because we want them, but rather because we want them in order to serve Hashem. Based upon this teaching of the Zohar, R. Chaim of Volozhin is said to have avoided asking for anything personal on Rosh Hashanah in his prayers,[8] and indeed many consider this the appropriate mode of behavior. Must we indeed refrain from asking God for health, wealth, and peace of mind in our prayers over Rosh Hashanah?

Imagine a builder hired by a king to build the new palace. If he uses his new position to continually ask the king for special treatment and personal favors, the king's patience will wear thin. But in another scenario, that same builder could ask for much more, and stay in the king's good graces. Should he ask the king for the materials needed to build the palace that the king ordered him to build, surely that is appropriate. A person who approaches Hashem asking for all sorts of personal things, but with the orientation toward doing Hashem's will, is not doing something selfish at all. When a mother says, "Hashem, give me the energy and patience to raise beautiful children, who will bring Torah and happiness and goodness to the world," that is not selfish. When a person says, "Please give me enough money to have the financial means and worry free disposition to properly raise a family that can spread Torah values and care for the needy, and allow me to still have time to study Torah in a way that will truly help me to be an even better servant of Yours," that

---

8. Cited in *Kovetz Halachos, Yamim Noraim* p. 99, n. 9. See there for a comprehensive approach to asking for personal things on Rosh Hashanah.

is not selfish.[9] The person who makes sure that he has what he needs in order to be most effective in life cannot be considered selfish if his life is about much more than just himself.

Our requests from Hashem during these precious days are not meant to be selfish, for that is the way that a dog might ask. They are meant to be about idealism, and devotion to Hashem. We want so much, and we need so much, but we do not have to fear, for when Hashem is *maoz chayai*—the strength and center of my life—then I can know that no matter how things turn out, I will have just what I need.

By orienting ourselves with Hashem as our compass, we can embark on a journey of growth more magnificent and far-reaching than anything we have ever thought possible.

---

9. This point was made by R. Yisrael Salanter, see R. Dessler's *Michtav Me-Eliyahu* Vol. 4, p. 269, in the essay, "The World is a High-Priced Hotel."

2

It Is *They* Who Stumble and Fall

בִּקְרֹב עָלַי מְרֵעִים לֶאֱכֹל אֶת בְּשָׂרִי
צָרַי וְאֹיְבַי לִי הֵמָּה כָשְׁלוּ וְנָפָלוּ:

*My tormentors and enemies against me, it is
they who stumble and fall.*

R. Shmuel Laniado explains[10] that David noticed that his enemies wound up falling in the very traps that they set for him. The wickedness present inside of his enemies wound up hurting nobody else but them.

The Sweat of the Angels

The river *di nur*,[11] teaches the Gemara,[12] is produced by the sweat of the *Chayos* angels, and Rav Zutra bar Tovia cited

10. *Teruas Melech* to *Tehillim* 27, s.v. *shema tomar*. R. Shmuel Laniado, also known as *Baal ha-Kelim* was Rabbi in Aleppo in the later part of the 16th century.
11. See Daniel 7:10.
12. *Chagigah* 13b.

Rav as teaching that it empties on the heads of the wicked in *gehinnom* (purgatory). Rema Mi-Fano explains that the *Chayos* are the angels who hold up Hashem's Throne of Glory.[13] Generally, lifting spiritual things is easy. In fact, the Ark of the Covenant carried those who lifted it, actually giving them strength and assistance.[14] The spiritual things that we take on our shoulders actually grant us strength. But the *Chayos* were sweating, because preserving Hashem's honor is hard in the face of sin and evil actions. When people act in wickedness, then a look at the world does not appear to reveal Hashem's presence, but instead, makes Him appear to be absent, and it is a mighty battle to uphold His Throne of Honor and Glory in the face of apparent dishonor. It is that very sweat, which the wicked people caused with their actions, that falls upon them in *gehinnom*. They are the ones who ultimately pay the price for the trouble that they caused.

The penalty for wickedness is nothing more than consequences, reaping what was sowed. When one lives a life of goodness, we are taught that it is not appropriate to do so simply in order to receive reward.[15] How absurd would it be if someone saved his own child from drowning in order to secure a lollypop, or even a car! A person who could possibly be motivated to save his child's life by the promise of anything material is a person who fails to appreciate the value of the relationship for its own sake. We need to value our connection to Hashem not because

13. *Chikur Din* 3:2. See also *Shaarei Leshem* 1, 15:1.
14. *Sotah* 35a.
15. *Avos* 1:3.

of some abstract reward, but out of the awareness that doing the mitzvos is its own reward. It is the ultimate reward—connection and oneness with Hashem.

The Blessing *Is* the Listening

The punishment for evil will be the very results of that evil. And the reward for good is also not something separate. When the Torah speaks of the blessing that will come to the Jewish people if they keep the mitzvos, it says, "...the blessing that you will keep the mitzvos."[16] We would think it should have said, "the blessing *if* you will keep..." The word "*that*," says the *Panim Yafos*,[17] teaches us that the blessing is really the mitzvah itself, with any other blessing of riches or health as a side benefit.

This awareness leads King David to ask, in the coming verses, for nothing at all other than to sit in the House of Hashem, for that is goodness: a deep and passionate relationship with Hashem. The awareness that our desire to misbehave does not and cannot lead us to happiness or fulfillment is the beginning of our wake-up call, leading up to Rosh Hashanah and Yom Kippur. The wicked people fall into traps that they themselves have set. This message is one that we would do well to inculcate in ourselves, as we set our sights on higher and loftier goals.

---

16. *Devarim* 11:27.

17. *Panim Yafos, Tinyana* to *Re'eh*. For more on this, see *Panim Yafos, Acharei Mos* 16:29, p. 269 in Gross ed., and note how he ties it in to our chapter of *Tehillim*. See also *Devarim Rabbah* 4:3, as well as *Ha-Torah ha-Temimah* (Stern) to *Eichah* 3:38 (p. 269) citing the *Ohel Yaakov* who elaborates on this point, and explains, in light of it, the nature of all mitzvos and the reward that results in observing them.

3

A Course in Obstacles

אִם תַּחֲנֶה עָלַי מַחֲנֶה לֹא יִירָא לִבִּי
אִם תָּקוּם עָלַי מִלְחָמָה בְּזֹאת אֲנִי בוֹטֵחַ׃

Though an army would besiege me, my heart would not fear;
though war would arise against me, in this I trust.

Enemies

Hebrew grammar, if speaking about one's enemy, would
normally dictate that the words be: *im yachaneh alai machaneh*,
which would mean, "if [the enemy] would send an army against
me...." The word *tachaneh* is unusual.[18]

The Midrash[19] may offer us an answer to this question, albeit
without addressing it head on, when it says, "The Jewish people

---

18. See R. Hirsch, who notes this in his comments to this verse, and
suggests an approach.
19. *Yalkut Shimoni* to *Tehillim* 27:706.

said to Hashem, 'If You send against me an enemy…'" The word *tachaneh* makes sense if we are speaking directly to Hashem, telling Him, "If You send an army against me, I will not fear…."

Hashem Sent Them

The enemy we face is, indeed, frightening. One great key that King David is showing us is that we should learn to see that Hashem is the One Who sends us our challenges—instead of seeing them as coming directly from our enemies. If it's Hashem Who is sending us our hardship, then our hearts need not fear.

Five *Alefs* in a Row

"The enemy said, 'I will chase, catch them, and divide their spoils,'"[20] says the Torah when speaking of the Egyptians as they planned their chase of the Jewish people, who were then en route to the Red Sea. As we all know, something else was to unfold, and those enemies were never really going to hurt us after all. R. Yaakov Yosef of Polonye, in his *Toldos Yaakov Yosef*,[21] records a teaching that he heard from the Baal Shem Tov about this verse. In the Torah, the verse reads, *amar oyev erdof assig achalek*, with five words in a row beginning with the first letter of the Hebrew alphabet, *alef*. The *alef*, explained the Baal Shem Tov, represents Hashem, the One and only, Master of the world. In Hebrew an *aluf* is a leader, or person occupying a position of importance.[22] Hashem is *Alufo shel Olam*, the Leader of this world. This verse tells us that even in the actions of the enemy,

---

20. *Shemos* 15:5.
21. To *Bereshis* 1. See also his comments to *Vayeshev* 6.
22. See *Bereshis* 26:15–19.

we are to see Hashem's presence. His plan is being carried out, and we are heading to miracles like splitting seas, even when we seem only to have an enemy facing us.

Inside the Snake

A similar teaching is found in the work *Maateh Tehillah*[23] by Rabbi Yaakov Rokeach of Tripoli (1800-1891), to explain a verse in *Tehillim*: "The wicked man waits in ambush for the righteous... Hashem will not forsake him to his hand...."[24] He cites an earlier work, *Shem Shmuel*,[25] who observes that when the word *nachash*, "serpent," is spelled out in its *milui* form, where all letters are spelled out fully, the middle letters are the same value as Hashem's name. This means that though the word *nachash* is really made up of only three letters, a *nun*, *ches*, and *shin*, each of those letters, when spelled out themselves, read as three words: The letter *nun* is spelled using the letters *nun*, *vav*, and then another *nun*; *ches* is spelled with a *ches*, *yod*, and *tav*; and finally, there is the *shin*, spelled *shin*, *yod*, *nun*. The middle three letters of each of these spelled-out letters add up to 26, which is the value of Hashem's name. For at the heart of the approaching wicked man is Hashem, Who is in the middle of it all, and He does not let things get out of His control.

No Revenge

When a person mistreats another person, the Torah warns the victim against taking revenge.[26] The reason, explains the *Sefer*

---

23. To *Tehillim* 37:32, p. 39.
24. Vv. 37:32–33.
25. P. 4a.
26. *Vayikra* 19:18.

ha-Chinnuch,[27] is "so that a man can know, and truly take to heart, that all things that befall him, from good to evil, have reason to befall him from Hashem. No man can do anything to another man without the will of Hashem present. Therefore, when a person hurts him, he can know in his heart that it was his own shortcomings that caused a negative decree to come upon him, and he should thus refrain from focusing his attention on revenge, since that person is not even really the true cause of his trouble; his sins were. As King David said, "Let him curse, for Hashem told him to curse,"[28] blaming it all on his own sins, rather than on Shimi ben Gera, the man cursing him.

In other words, though we certainly believe that man is blessed with free will, at the same time, we see the Divine hand guiding one's life, to the point that no person can be harmed without Hashem wishing that person to receive that experience, and message. Though certainly, the sinner will be punished for harming another person, that fact is something that can take one away from introspection. Our job is to see Hashem as the precise orchestrator of each of our troubles. If we focus all of our attention on our enemies, reviewing their evil characteristics in our head, and thinking only about how wicked and sinful they are, though we may be correct, we are squandering a wonderful opportunity in our quest for achievement. Instead, we are to direct that energy inward, and we must let go of the desire for revenge—as deserving of it as another person may be—and do our very best to discover the divine message tucked away in all of this.

---

27. Mitzvah 241.
28. *Shmuel* II 16:11.

Hashem Is My Light

As we approach Rosh Hashanah and Yom Kippur, there is a great deal of focus on our relationships with Hashem, and with other people. We ask others for forgiveness, and we grant others the same. As we look at those who have harmed us, and any obstacles that we have faced, let us resolve to direct our speech to Hashem, and say, "If You, Hashem, send an army against me, I will not fear that army at all, for You are right here with me. I will fear only You, Hashem, and I will trust that there is meaning, growth, and achievement for me to extract from this experience."

4

I Ask One Thing –
and Here's the List!

אַחַת שָׁאַלְתִּי מֵאֵת ה׳ אוֹתָהּ אֲבַקֵּשׁ שִׁבְתִּי בְּבֵית ה׳
כָּל יְמֵי חַיַּי לַחֲזוֹת בְּנֹעַם ה׳ וּלְבַקֵּר בְּהֵיכָלוֹ :

I have asked one thing from Hashem, that I sit in the house
of Hashem all my life, that I see the pleasantness of Hashem,
and that I visit His sanctuary.

The Midrash[29] records that Hashem remarked to King David, "First you said that you are asking for just one thing, and then you went and asked for a whole list of things!" To which King David replied, "I learned from You, Hashem! Should a servant

---

29. *Shocher Tov* 27, *Yalkut Shimoni* to *Tehillim* 706.

not emulate his Master? For You said,[30] 'And now, Israel, what does God ask of you after all? Just to fear God,' and then You went on to include an abundance of mitzvos, as it says there, 'to follow in all of His ways.'"

Though superficially, this answer sounds clever, it requires further understanding. What does King David's deceptive sounding laundry list of requests have to do with Hashem's request that we only fear Him, followed by His subsequent addition of all the other commandments to the request?

The answer lies in a more nuanced understanding of the mitzvos.

Being Scattered

"Hashem, your God, will afflict the enemies who stand up to you; they will come out to attack you on one path, and down seven paths they will flee from you."[31] If the Jewish people keep the Torah, and live as they should, then Hashem promises that all sorts of blessings will come to them. Among them is the blessing that their enemies will flee from them if and when they attack. The Torah tells us, fascinatingly, that they will flee in seven directions. Rashi explains, "it is the way of frenzied people to flee in a scattered way."[32] Unity is a product of organization and peace; chaos makes people frenzied and order-less. But having those people scatter in seven directions is

---

30. *Devarim* 10:12.
31. *Devarim* 28:7.
32. To *Devarim* 28:7, s.v. *uvshiva.*

interesting. After all, are there only seven ways that the enemies might flee? Why does the Torah employ the imagery of seven different paths?

The Seven-Headed Serpent

Our Sages teach us a great deal about the *yetzer hara*—the part inside of every human that urges him or her to make bad choices, and to favor what is more comfortable or attractive over what is right and good. One thing they tell us is that the *yetzer hara* has seven different names.[33] In one amazing story,[34] they paint the picture of the *yetzer hara* as a serpent with seven different heads. We are told that this serpent terrorized the villagers of a certain town, and it was only when Rav Acha bar Yaakov was duped into entering the synagogue where that serpent-demon was present that the serpent was demolished. Rav Acha vanquished this demon by praying to Hashem, and each time he bowed himself to Hashem, another one of the serpent's heads fell off until the seventh bow took off the demon's last head, and he was no more.[35] While this cryptic teaching is surely packed with secrets

33. *Sukkah* 52a.
34. *Kiddushin* 29b.
35. Note the comments of *Panim Yafos* (*Bereshis* 32:29, pp. 100–101 in Mishor ed.), where he speaks of how Yaakov bowed to Esav seven times, thus turning the Satan, who is associated with the angel and power of Esav, into something good, and breaking the power of the Satan, who is the *yetzer hara* and has seven names. He also makes the connection to the seven bows of R. Acha that we are speaking of here. The *Panim Yafos* also wrote a work called *Sefer ha-Mikneh*, in which he echoes this teaching (*Kiddushin, ad loc.*). See also the important piece of *Megalleh Amukos* (*Va'Eschanan* 192), where he elaborates upon this as well, and explains the interaction of Yaakov and Esav in light of this story of Rav Acha.

that are beyond my comprehension,[36] true things can always be understood on many levels, and perhaps there is something meaningful that we can glean from this amazing episode.

Being scattered is something that every human being deals with. Work, family, religion, and leisure activities all jostle for position in our lives. Ideally, one's life would enjoy a unity of purpose that ties disparate parts together into one organic unit. The builder of a home may have many tasks: carpets, windows, landscaping, and roofing, but his task is one task and one task only. He is building a home. The same is meant to be true in our lives. We have to eat, sleep, work, play, and learn, but all of these are merely parts of one whole. We are here to achieve; to single-mindedly work to fill the world with goodness and light by fulfilling the Torah and doing the will of Hashem. Anything else that we need to do in this life is simply a branch of that task. The part of us that gets distracted, the *yetzer hara*, is the part of us that gets us to focus on specific things at the expense of other things. It encourages us to seek immediate fulfillment rather than lasting happiness. We feel pulled to relax not in order to achieve more in the scheme of things by resting, but rather as an end in and of itself. One who follows the *yetzer hara* will have as much direction and unity as a creature with seven different heads, each trying to pull the extremities and resources in its intended direction.

---

36. See the comments of *Noda bi-Yehudah* in his introduction to his commentary on the Talmud, the *Tzlach*, where he explains that many of the cryptic messages of our sages cannot be comprehended in their entirety in this life.

That's Not a Name!

We mentioned that the *yetzer hara* has seven different names. We are also taught that the angel of Esav is identified with the *yetzer hara, they are the very same entity.*[37] The angel of Esav fought with Yaakov, and when Yaakov conquered him, then asked him his name, he responded, "Why do you ask my name?"[38]

Rabbi Leib Chasman once explained that this was not a deflection, but rather the actual name of the angel.[39] His proper name was, "Why do you ask my name"! The very nature of the forces of distraction is that they simply have no identity; there is no single, unified purpose—no name. The great advantage of the meaningful life is the unity that it offers. One of the most frustrating things that one can witness in another person is a lack of unity. Hypocrisy. It is so hard to watch someone who presents himself as religious and pious being rude to another person. When a great proponent of marriage and faithfulness is found guilty of infidelity, we are less than enchanted. When a very public advocate devoting his life to fighting global warming and encouraging others to use limited energy is found to be using, in his home and with his jet, more than twelve times what the average person uses in his country, it's so distressing! But that is the nature of the challenge that our lives present us. We

---

37. His name is Samael, and he is identified with the Satan. See Rambam in *Moreh Nevuchim* 2:30. Satan is another name for the *yetzer hara*, see *Bava Basra* 16a.
38. *Bereshis* 32:30.
39. Cited by R. Eliezer Schach, in a discourse printed in *Yeshurun* Vol. 11, p. 460. The same idea is cited in the *Likkutei Basar Likkutei* to *Bereshis, ad loc.* from the *Mar Dror.*

are enjoined to be unified, and when we are so, our enemies and challenges will reveal themselves to be scattered and irrelevant.

"Cleave to God,"[40] demands the Torah. "But can one, in fact, cleave to the Divine?" wonders the Talmud.[41] Rather, says the Talmud, this teaches us to cleave to the wise, do business with them, eat and drink with them, and marry into their families. The Rambam[42] explains that this is what our Sages meant when they said, "Scuffle in the dirt of their feet, and drink their words thirstily."[43] That is how you connect to the Divine!

Isn't this fascinating? There is no talk in the *Gemara* about attending their classes, just about eating with them and doing business with them. For, the greatness of Torah is manifest primarily when it extends to the entire person. When a person is truly spiritual, he becomes more kind. His business associates know that he is a better person as a boss, coworker, or employee, just as the person who sits near him when he prays can see that he is serious about his prayer. True spirituality spreads and makes a difference on the whole person. *Kiddush Hashem* is exemplified when a person demonstrates in his life that his connection to the Divine, to God, has made him a better person. This occurs, we are taught, when those who interact with him exclaim, "How fortunate must his parents and Rabbis be, who taught him Torah."[44] When a person from the outside

---

40. *Devarim* 11:22, 30:20.
41. *Kesuvos* 111b.
42. *Deʾos* 6:2.
43. *Avos* 1:4.
44. *Yoma* 86a.

can see that it was the message of Torah, Judaism, and Truth that propelled this person to his great levels in human kindness and sensitivity, that is *Kiddush Hashem*. When they can see his greatness as a product of Torah, even when it is in an area that appears far from "spiritual," that is the definition of displaying the inherent holiness in Hashem's Torah.

There are seven ways that space is defined in traditional Jewish thought. Up, down, the four directions of the compass, and where you are right now. There is nothing more. Seven. The *yetzer hara* has seven names, for he pulls you in every single direction of the world. The demon's heads are shattered when one bows to Hashem, when one commits his life to doing what is right, always, and with all of his abilities. Not just in the shul, but even out of the shul. Perhaps this demon appeared in a shul to teach us that lesson. If your spirituality is limited to the synagogue, and does not extend to the rest of your life, then you must kill some of the demon's heads. The best way to do so is to bow down[45]—to subject your whole life to the Truth, and to the values that you recognize. Know that Hashem is in charge of it all and that in life, it's all important, not just certain

---

45. See Maharsha to *Kiddushin* there (s.v. *kitanina*), where he shows that the power of bowing is the very opposite of the power of the serpent, as our Sages teach that after one bows, "He should stand upright like a serpent." Thus, we see that standing in a bowing position is not serpent-like. We therefore are taught in *Bava Kamma* 16a that anyone who fails to bow in thanks to Hashem during the *Modim* prayer will have his spine turned into a snake seven years after his death. He also talks about the seven negative powers of impurity that the serpent of Eden brought into the world, and that these are manifest in the seven names of the *yetzer hara*.

parts of it. You have to love scuffling in the dirt produced by the feet of the wise people. For that dirt is not just dirt, it's holy. Enjoy the dirt that your children produce when they walk in your home. Enjoy the dirty dishes that your guests add to your already busy schedule. These are all fantastic signs of spiritual achievement—nothing gets done without a mess. And perhaps, we will learn one of the deepest messages of the Torah: that the business and eating and cleaning up that wise people do are not disconnected parts of their lives that they must "get through" in order to get to the "real" part. We must take to our hearts that these distant things are actually part and parcel of a life well lived—cogs in the machinery of greatness. We need not suffer from the frenzied frustration of having seven bickering heads any longer. All of our lives can be driven by one mission, one head, and one heart, as our sages beautifully would say, "Just as a palm tree has but one heart, so do the Jewish people have but one heart focused on their Father in Heaven."[46]

Back to King David

David was asking for a life un-scattered. He was recognizing that one request of Hashem is all that is needed. To dedicate one's

---

46. *Sukkah* 45b. See also *Brachos* 57a: "One who sees a palm branch in his dream [is being informed that he] only has one heart toward his Father in Heaven." See *Leket Perushei Aggadah* (*ad loc.*, s.v. *kappos*), where he explains the imagery of a palm tree. Date palms, he writes, get very, very large in one direction only. They grow up, while their leaves do not spread out all that much, in contrast to most other trees. This represents a person who reaches upward to Hashem, with no interest in spreading himself in any other directions. See also *Teshuvos Mahari Weil* 191, and my comments in *Birchasa ve-Shirasa* to *Brachos*, *ad loc.*, s.v. *ha-roeh lulav.*

life to Hashem is something that will have myriad applications and bring much guidance and shelter from Hashem. But it's no more than one thing. He learned this from Hashem Himself, Who demanded only one thing: "fear of Hashem," or, as we might put it, a relationship with Hashem. To view Hashem with awe and reverence and live a life devoted to His ideals. That is all that Hashem wants, that simple choice.[47] Certainly, that will fuel observance of all the mitzvos. But they will not be separate and disconnected things. They will be manifold manifestations of one commitment.

As we approach our days of reflection, and figure out where our lives are headed, we juggle so much. We are parents, children, spouses, employers and employees, community members, and citizens. We need to find the glue that keeps it all connected and together, to see that Hashem is One, that we seek to live in His house, and find shelter in His shadow. We need desperately to learn that it is all one—and that we are really searching for but one thing.

---

47. The *Kadosh mi-Lublin*, cited by *Yitav Panim*, brought in *Likkutei Basar Likkutei* to *Devarim* 10:12, writes that the secret to this simple thing is hinted to in the words "and now Israel," which is how the verse begins. He explains that when a man knows that yesterday is gone, and tomorrow is far off, then he can learn to focus on what is right in front of him, and if he looks at just what is in front of him now, each decision is but a small thing, and it's not all that hard. After all, not smoking for a day, just right now, is certainly more manageable than "never smoking again for thousands of days"!

5

On the Rock

כִּי יִצְפְּנֵנִי בְּסֻכֹּה בְּיוֹם רָעָה יַסְתִּרֵנִי בְּסֵתֶר אָהֳלוֹ בְּצוּר יְרוֹמְמֵנִי :

*That He conceal me in His sukkah on a day of evil, and conceal
me in the inside of his tent, He will raise me up on a rock.*

The Rock Advantage

One has to wonder what sort of rock King David was hoping
to be placed upon by Hashem. Malbim[48] explains that he was
hoping to be out of his enemies' reach, as if he were up high on
a rock, beyond their grasp. *Metzudos*[49] explains that he wanted
to have the advantage of height, since one who is at the higher
point in battle has a distinct advantage. David wanted the
advantage over the forces that battled him.

But other sources suggest something more as well. Avraham
Avinu was a *tzur*, a rock, said Isaiah,[50] and so were the rest of the

---

48. *Tehillim* 27:5, *Biur ha-Inyan.*
49. *Ad loc.*
50. *Yeshaya* 51:1–2.

Avos.[51] King David was looking to connect to his ancestors—Avraham, Yitzchak, and Yaakov—explains the *Chesed Le-Avraham*,[52] for this offered him the advantage he needed, and the protection from his enemies.

This is, indeed, a theme that we often see in Torah practice; we even refer to Hashem as the God of Avraham, Yitzchak, and Yaakov in our personal prayer.[53] What is the nature of this connection, and why is it so vital?

Doing Your Job

"Not with you alone, do I seal this covenant… but with those who are standing with us here today, and with those who are not here with us today."[54] Hashem made a deal with the Jewish people, both with those present and those who were not there. Targum Yonason[55] explains that all the souls that would be born in the future were present at that covenant, as well as those who lived in the past. One wonders what sort of covenant might be made with those who have already lived!

---

51. Rashi to *Bemidbar* 23:9, s.v. *ki me-rosh tzurim.*
52. By son of Tiferes Shlomo of Radomsk to *Sukkos* 31b, s.v. *Tehillim.* See also this approach by the Maggid of Pollachok, printed in *Yeshurun* Vol. 4, p. 359. See also *Eretz ha-Chaim* to *Tehillim* 61, p. 112, also cited in *Otzar Tehillos Yisrael* Vol. 7 on *Tehillim* 61, p. 420.
53. *Chiddushei ha-Rim*, cited by his grandson *Sfas Emes*, in many places (*Lech Lecha* 5635, s.v. *Be-Midrash Anochi*; *Tazria* 5631, s.v. *achor ve-kedem*; Chanukah 5633, s.v. *leil gimmel* and many many others), explains that *Magen Avraham* means that God promises that He will protect a little piece of Abraham that will be present in every single Jew, and can never be destroyed.
54. *Devarim* 29:13–14.
55. *Devarim* 29:13–14, see also Targum Yerushalmi *ad loc.*

R. Menachem Azaria of Fano[56] explains that by including them in this covenant along with all the Jews who lived then, and would live eventually, they benefited in that now they would each be considered as a "commanded one who fulfilled mitzvos." The *Gemara*[57] teaches us that one who does things that he is responsible for doing, has done something even greater than the person who has done other things that are beyond the call of duty. Surely, it's laudable to do extra things on top of one's obligations, but one must first feed his own family, before he goes out to feed others. One can know what is most important for him to fulfill in his life not by looking to the edges of the earth for extra-credit opportunities, but rather by looking to fulfill his obligations.

The child is not expected to support a family, and take responsibility for others. But as he grows, he reaches a level where this is expected of him. So is it with a nation of people. Those who lived in Israel's infancy period were not part of a nation with any real responsibility, but as they entered the land of Israel, they became a nation with responsibilities, a much more lofty and mature role. Those who lived before were now part of a people with responsibilities, and retroactively, their achievement became more important, so they were there for this momentous occasion.

The Secret of the *Chasam Sofer*
"God, why is it that the Jews don't sing *Shirah* [the song of joy and praise to Hashem usually sung on holidays] on Rosh

56. *Maamar ha-Nefesh* 4:13.
57. *Kiddushin* 31a.

Hashanah?" asked the angels. God responded, "Can it be that a king would sit in justice, with the books of the living and the dead open before him, and the Jews would nevertheless sing *Shirah*?" So taught Rabbi Abahu.[58]

The *Chasam Sofer*[59] lets us in on a secret that he was privy to. He was passed down the tradition that all holy souls of our ancestors who are no longer living come to the synagogue with us on Rosh Hashanah and Yom Kippur and join us in prayer.[60] Thus, he explains, the books of the living and the dead are, indeed, open before Hashem, in the sense that the dead are actually part of the High Holiday prayers. Since dead people cannot praise Hashem, as King David said,[61] thus Rosh Hashanah is not an appropriate time to sing *Shirah*, and only when the dead rise again will they sing a great song.

We learn that Rosh Hashanah is a time of sobriety, where we connect to our prayers in the context of all of history, with the dead right next to us, praying, as it were, for their lives to have meaning and fulfillment through our efforts in continuing their missions. Songs are for when we are at a summit, when we are finished with a great task: "Those who plant in tears, reap in song!"[62] When the Jews crossed the Red Sea, and watched

---

58. *Arachin* 10b, *Rosh Hashanah* 32b.
59. *Drashos Chasam Sofer* 350b, s.v. *asher yeshno.*
60. See also Benayahu to *Rosh Hashanah* 16a, s.v. *kol ba'ei olam*, where he talks of how the dead are also judged on Rosh Hashanah, as to whether they need *gilgul*, and more.
61. *Tehillim* 115:17.
62. *Tehillim* 126:5.

their enemies die, and things reached their pinnacle, they sang *Shirah*. And when Moshiach comes, we will sing a great song, as the world reaches its great perfection. On our festivals, when we celebrate a spiritual gift, or great religious experience, we sing *Shirah*. But we do not sing *Shirah* on Rosh Hashanah, for there is much too much left to do. Dead people who did not bring the world to its perfection are still waiting to sing *Shirah*, for their task was not yet finished; the world is not yet perfect. On Rosh Hashanah, when we are assessed as a world, the dead are as present as those who are alive, in some way. All of mankind, from the beginning of time, is being judged by Hashem. How are we progressing in the journey from Creation, back in Eden, to Perfection, as the world is meant to be some day? And while we are in that mode, we do not focus on the joy of what we have done, but on the task ahead of us, and how we hope to complete that in the year to come.

We can therefore understand why it is that Yom Kippur must follow Rosh Hashanah. Though on some level, it would seem right to clean up our sins *before* the coronation of the King, and the fresh start of a new year, this is not so. For only once we get back in touch with the whole picture of history, and the connection that we have to all of mankind, only then can we have the clarity to reassess our methods and see where we can improve in the grand scheme of things. The days of *teshuvah* (repentance) that lead up to Yom Kippur are the direct outcome of Rosh Hashanah.

It is the people who lived long ago who are part of us. They really achieve when we achieve, since we are simply one long unit with them. And thus, they were present for our covenant, for it is their covenant. Their actions are having more and more impact, as we progress and grow and achieve.

Knock, Knock!

In our High Holiday prayers, we address Hashem as, "He Who opens the door to those who knock in *teshuvah*." The *Sfas Emes*[63] cited his grandfather, the *Chiddushei Ha-Rim*, who explained that "those who knock in *teshuvah*" are Avraham, Yitzchak, and Yaakov. They opened the door for *teshuvah*, for mankind to return to its destiny, and for people to get back to where they should be. It is through our connection to them, explains the *Sfas Emes*, that we can properly do *teshuvah*. And so they come to join us. They are present with us on the High Holidays. They join us, to remind us that the work that we are doing is merely a continuation of the work that the great nation that we are part of has been doing as we have marched through history. We are all in the new year together—so much depends upon us. It is not yet time to sing that great *Shirah*, for we are not quite there—but that time is coming soon, and then we will all sing together; for, even those who we do not see in the shul are there with us in spirit. They opened the doors for us to scoot through long ago, and in some way, they are there encouraging us, praying for us, and urging us forward, in our most important times.

---

63. *Sfas Emes, Shabbos Shuvah* 5636, s.v. *be-shem*. See also *Lech Lecha* 5658, s.v. *be-midrash achos*; *Va'era* 5662, s.v. *isa be-midrash*.

King David knew that his success was but a part of a larger scheme of things. He asked Hashem to please place him up on a rock, to connect his life to the lives of his illustrious ancestors. This is a lesson we must all connect with as we approach the Days of Awe.

6

The Glorious Sound of *Teruah*

וְעַתָּה יָרוּם רֹאשִׁי עַל אֹיְבַי סְבִיבוֹתַי וְאֶזְבְּחָה בְאָהֳלוֹ
זִבְחֵי תְרוּעָה אָשִׁירָה וַאֲזַמְּרָה לַה':

*Now my head is raised above my enemies around me and I will
slaughter offerings in his tent accompanied by teruah [joyous
song]; I will sing and chant praise to Hashem.*

Songs of *Teruah*

The *teruah* is a very important sound in Jewish thought. There
is a holiday known as *Yom Teruah*[64] in the Torah. We are
accustomed to calling it Rosh Hashanah; but its true character
is the day of shofar blasts, specifically, apparently, the sort of
broken blast called the *teruah*. There is something special about
this blast and its spiritual effects. But what is it, and why does
it show up here, when King David is raising his head whilst
surrounded by enemies?

---

64. *Bemidbar* 29:1.

R. Samson Raphael Hirsch[65] explains this verse as coming from David's mouth long before he succeeded in vanquishing his foes. He was saying, "Even while surrounded by enemies, I have confidence that Hashem will save me, so much so that I can offer *zivchei teruah*, with joyous song, already!" A similar sentiment is expressed by King David elsewhere[66] when he says, "With gratitude and praise I call out to Hashem, and from my enemies I will be saved." Rashi explains these words to mean,[67] "Even before the salvation, I praise Hashem for it, for I am absolutely confident that He will save me from my enemies!" The songs of *teruah*, then, are being offered during the troubling times,[68] expressing a joy and conviction that one is under the watchful eye of a benevolent God. But what does all this have to do with the nature of the *teruah* blast specifically, and the shofar of Rosh Hashanah?

Musical Chairs

"Fortunate is the nation who knows[69] the *teruah*," teaches the verse.[70] The Midrash[71] wonders, is Israel the only nation who can make music? Do other nations not have all sorts of symphonies?

65. Commentary to Psalms, 27:6.
66. *Tehillim* 18:4.
67. *Tehillim, ad loc.*, s.v. *mehullal.* See also *Shmuel* II 22:4 and Rashi, *ad loc.*
68. See Ramban to *Bereshis* 19:8, who understands the *zivchei teruah* of our verse to be what one offers after he is saved, to express gratitude to Hashem and announce His great deeds to others. Indeed, to have such emotion in the dire time itself is no small feat.
69. See *Iyun Yaakov* to *Sotah* 5a for an alternative rendering of *yodei*, to mean not "knowing," but "wailing"!
70. *Tehillim* 89:16.
71. *Vayikra Rabbah* 29:3.

Rather, the verse is telling us that Israel is fortunate to grasp the mystery of how to please Hashem with the *teruah*, causing Hashem to get up from His Throne of Justice, and move to His Throne of Mercy. Hashem then is filled with feelings of mercy toward Israel, and Hashem's justice is converted to mercy.

R. Shimon Greenfield,[72] the *Maharshag*, explains this somewhat esoteric-sounding teaching. One of the teachers of Rabbi Akiva was called Nachum Ish Gamzu.[73] No matter what happened

---

72. *Zehav Sheva*, *Mo'adim*, Rosh Hashanah, p. 1.

73. See Rema Mi-Fano's *Gilgulei Neshamos*, where he asserts that Nachum Ish Gamzu was a reincarnation of Lot. Thus, in *Taanis* 21a, a miracle is done to the dirt of Nachum Ish Gamzu in the very same way that the miracle occurred for Avraham whilst saving his nephew Lot. And just like when Lot left Sodom, it immediately was destroyed, so it was with Nachum Ish Gamzu: as soon as he left the house, it collapsed. Regarding Nachum Ish Gamzu, it says that in the morning, when he saw that it was dirt and not jewels, he said, *gam zu le-tovah*, "this too is for the good," and proceeded to the Caesar. [See Maharsha and *Gevuros Ari* (s.v. *le-machar*), who suggest an alternative text. Maharal (*Nesivos Olam*, *Nesiv ha-Bitachon* 1) writes that, indeed, he knew, but his faith in Hashem was so outstanding that he was certain that nothing bad would happen and that it would all be for the best! See this theme also regarding praying effectively, that it brings someone to a state where no bad happens to them all day (*Brachos* 9b). Rabbeinu Yonah (*Brachos* 2b in *dappei ha-Rif*) and Ritva 4b, citing Rabbeinu Yonah, write that praying properly by connecting *geulah* to *tefillah* (the Shema to the *Shemoneh Esrei*) is about faith in Hashem. For, explains Maharal in *Nesivos Olam* (*Nesiv ha-Avodah* 9), through a person leaving the control of others (*geulah*), he can be free to enter Hashem's service, *tefillah*. See R. Tzadok of Lublin (*Pri Tzaddik*, Lag Ba'Omer 4), who says, "This certainly is not just about words, but about a deep intellectual awareness." The sign that one prayed properly with the connecting of *geulah le-tefillah* is when a smile never leaves his face that whole day, says the Talmud. Just like Nachum Ish Gamzu, that person who brings himself under Hashem's control will have a wonderful day no matter what comes his way.

to him, he would always insist that it, too, was for the best.[74] Indeed, he was always correct; things did turn out for the best. A great method to turn harsh circumstances into positive ones, explains *Maharshag*, is to do what Nachum Ish Gamzu did, and exude absolute confidence that things were, indeed, for the best.

One should say this aloud, and remind himself that Hashem is the source of all good things, and that though it may be perplexing at the moment, it is certainly for the absolute best. We are to chalk up the confusing parts of Hashem's behavior to our poor vision, and when we do this, amazingly, the negative challenges will flip around into positive things. Suddenly, it will be something that we can actually see, rather than an abstract article of faith. The spiritual result of true confidence that things are all for the best is the revelation to all that indeed, it was for the best all along. A person must make a blessing on negative things, should they occur, with the same joy[75] as when positive things occur.[76] And when he does this, recognizing that if something is Hashem's will, then it's right and worthy of joy, he actually affects the world in such a way that no longer is Hashem in need of sending anything that appears angry or negative, and immediately we can see the goodness therein.

"I praised You, Hashem, when You were angry at me, Your anger was gone and You consoled me," said Yeshaya.[77] Explains

---

74. *Taanis* 21a.
75. Rambam, *Hilchos Brachos* 10:3.
76. *Brachos* 49a, *Shulchan Aruch, Orach Chaim* 200.
77. *Yeshaya* 12:1.

Maharshag, once Yeshaya expressed his confidence in the inherent goodness of what Hashem was doing for him, he immediately merited to see that very goodness.[78]

Broken Sounds

The word *teruah* itself means "broken." It can even be used in the context of breaking something or someone.[79] The praise that we offer Hashem with the *teruah*, explains *Maharshag*, is the gratitude that we have to Hashem even during the tough times. One who has a fundamentally distrustful relationship with another person may feel kindly disposed to him or her, as long as they are being treated well, but the moment something appears out of order, they will likely not give much thought to the notion that it is the other who is blinded. But when one trusts another so fully that he is confident that what the other person is doing is entirely in his best interest, no matter how impossible it seems, that is a trustful relationship. Relating to Hashem that way is something uniquely Jewish. Other nations have no such relationship with Hashem. The ability to sing the songs of *teruah*, a broken call, from a seemingly broken person, who refuses to capitulate to suffering and sadness and clings to a belief that he is from the chosen people and enjoys a loving relationship with God—that is the Jewish way.

---

78. See *Maharshag* there, who also uses this concept to explain *Tehillim* 118:21, *odecha ki anisani va-tihi li li-yeshua*, "The praise that I offered when I you impoverished me was itself the salvation for me."
79. See *Tehillim* 2:9, *tero'em be-shevet barzel*, and *Yeshaya* 24:19.

The Amazing History of David's Harp

King David suffered but sang to Hashem. His are the songs of *teruah*. We are taught by our Sages[80] that, fascinatingly, the harp of King David was made up of strings that came from the sinews of the ram that Avraham Avinu offered at the *Akeidah*! For, Avraham, in the toughest of times, taught us that even if it appears that you are being asked to slaughter your child, if it is Hashem asking you, it is far more likely that you are blind to what is really happening, than that Hashem is being cruel! Whether one is inclined to understand that David's harp strings were, indeed, literally from that ram,[81] or if one takes a more allegorical view; one can know beyond any shadow of a doubt that the sounds of the ram that Avraham offered were sounds of faith and conviction that Hashem has it right!

Avraham was the first convert.[82] He was the one who recognized that he was a stranger among people, and that Hashem was really

---

80. *Pirkei de-Rabbi Eliezer* 31.

81. See *Shut Machaneh Efraim* (Vol. 3, *Yoreh Deah* 67 s.v. *ve-rayah*), who wonders how David was allowed to play such a harp when using the strings would seem to be prohibited under the restrictions of *me'ilah be-hekdesh*. See *Ein Eliyahu* to *Brachos* 3b, who explains that this is referring to the harp that hung above David's head, which the *Gemara* in *Brachos* asserts played on its own in the wind. This would mean that David's actual harp playing (see *Shmuel* I 16, and *Midrash Shocher Tov* 22) must have been done on other harps. Indeed, the whole idea of this question presumes that these body parts were not offered, but as Ramban points out (on *Shemos* 19:13), for an *olah* sacrifice as Avraham offered, all parts must be burnt. Thus, he explains that after they were offered, Hashem recreated them. Perhaps that is another answer to our question here, for one who is inclined to understand this in the most literal sense. Indeed, *Otzar Pelaos ha-Torah* to *Bereshis* (p. 307) suggests this answer.

82. *Sukkah* 49b.

there running the show.[83] The process of conversion, which makes one a child of Avraham, is described in the Talmud[84] and codified by the Rambam[85] as follows: "When a person comes to convert to Judaism, and upon investigation we see no ulterior motive, we ask him or her, 'What possesses you to convert? Do you not know that these days the Jewish people are sickly, pushed around, doubled over, ripped apart, and all sorts of suffering comes upon them?' If he or she responds, 'I know this and I don't deserve the privilege [of suffering as a Jew],' then we accept that person right away." No further questions are necessary. There is nothing more important in one's relationship with Hashem than this confidence. Becoming a Jew means joining the group that finds even the suffering in this world to be meaningful, and ultimately another manifestation of Divine goodness. This is how we crown Him as our King on Rosh Hashanah. Our confidence in His choices for our lives and for the fate of all the world is manifest in the sound of the shofar made of a ram's horn, which reminds us of the ram that Avraham offered at the Akeidah.[86]

---

83. *Bereshis Rabbah* 39:1 describes Avraham's incredulity at the possibility of a world without a creator, and how his life was defined as questioning this absurd premise, until the Creator revealed Himself. See also the involved approach of Netziv in his *Haamek She'elah, Ekev, Sheilta* 145 (p. 204) regarding how Avraham effected such a great change that Hashem actually became more involved in the world's affairs because of him! See also my *Birchasa ve-Shirasa* to *Brachos* 7b, s.v. *mi-yom she-bara*.

84. *Yevamos* 47a.

85. *Issurei Biah* 14:1.

86. *Rosh Hashanah* 16a: "Blow before Me a horn of a ram so that I will remember for you the ram of Isaac."

"One who recites the Hallel backwards," says the Talmud,[87] "has not fulfilled his obligation." The Hallel is a special prayer of gratitude to Hashem for the good that He does for us. The great Rabbi Yonason Shteiff[88] explained that this can be understood in light of a story in the Talmud elsewhere[89] of a fellow who intended to embark on a business journey by ship and was held up due to an injury causing him to miss the launch, causing him tremendous anguish. It was only when he learned of the tragic sinking of that ship that he then began to thank Hashem for the injury that precluded him from that journey. That man indeed said a Hallel of sorts, thanking his Creator for the good that befell him, but he only did so in retrospect, or "backwards." Once the whole story became clear, he said "thank you." Hallel is not fulfilled this way, but rather when one can have that level of sincere confidence in Hashem's salvation even before he is blessed with the clarity of vision to see how indeed it is for the best.[90] It is this level of relationship to which we aspire.

In the anonymous classic *Orchos Tzaddikim*, there is a section about trust in God, or *bitachon*. The chapter's title, surprisingly, is *Shaar ha-Simchah*, "Gate of Happiness," rather than "Gate of Trust." The *sefer* explains that one who has *bitachon* will always be in a state of happiness and joy, no matter what sort of

---

87. *Megillah* 17a.
88. Commentary to the Haggadah, p. 206, s.v. *Hallel*.
89. *Niddah* 31a.
90. See also the comment of R. Chaim Palagi in his *Chaim le-Rosh* to *Hagaddah shel Pesach*, *piska* 48 (p. 236 in Shuva Nafshi ed.) where he understands that the recitation of Hallel was itself the spiritual mechanism that freed the Jews from the grip of Pharaoh and brought them into Hashem's service.

challenge or tribulation he is faced with. A real relationship is one of trust and happiness so permeating and unshakable that everything else is illusory in comparison.

The word *teruah* comes from the word "broken," as does the word *ra*, "evil." And so does the word *reyah*, "friend"! Evil is the perception that things are broken, that the connection to Hashem is severed, and that things are not as they should be. Friends are two people who see themselves as broken from one another. They are, in reality, one, and simply two pieces that were separated.[91] Hashem is your best friend.[92] When you sound the *teruah* or hear its call, you are hearing the sounds of friendship and faith, and you can feel the greatest of optimism that things will be alright, for you are in the best of hands. The blast of the shofar on the Day of *Teruah* reminds us that our best bet is with Hashem. It is this orientation that causes Hashem to move Himself to the Throne of Mercy to bless us with eyes to see the benevolence being showered upon us every step of the way!

---

91. A *reyah* is a friend with whom one can connect on a deep level. See, for example, Ibn Ezra's comments to *Shemos* 21:35, s.v. *ve-chi yiggof*, where he disapprovingly cites the Karaite commentator Ben Zuta (a man who represented a movement not faithful to authentic Torah values), who understood that "his *reyah*" was speaking of another ox, as opposed to another person. After all, says Ibn Ezra, "The only meaningful friend that an ox could have would be Ben Zuta himself."
92. See Rashi to *Shabbos* 31a, s.v. *dialach sani*. He understands Hillel to be saying that this awareness, that Hashem is your best friend, is the most basic principle of the entire Torah. It is worth noting that this was Hillel's message to a prospective convert, for as we said earlier, this topic is the central lynchpin of the conversion process.

7

Hearing Voices

שְׁמַע ה' קוֹלִי אֶקְרָא וְחָנֵּנִי וַעֲנֵנִי :

Hashem, hear my voice when I call out;
be gracious to me and answer me.

Hashem hears not just the "voice," but the words too. The Spanish sage R. Yosef Yaavetz points this out in his fifteenth-century commentary to *Tehillim*,[93] questioning why David didn't ask Hashem to listen to his prayer, but instead to his voice.

Say What You Mean!

A great skill in life is to hear what someone is really saying. Imagine a sweet wife who just spent the day working, caring for children, and cleaning her home. Her husband comes home, sits down at the dinner table to a hot, home-cooked meal, and grumbles, "Noodles again?" This is not the way to treat your

---

93. *Chasid Yaavetz* to *Tehillim* 27:7.

wife. But, a discerning woman can sometimes understand that what he was really saying was, "I had such a hard day, I was not treated with respect at work, I just need someone to support me and love me for a few minutes now." There are many ways to say things, and many ways to hear things. The less sophisticated among us know what this is like—we have often expressed ourselves in unfortunate ways. The skill of listening to what is really being expressed is a crucial one. A person can be speaking sweetly and kindly, but attempting to swindle you. Another person can be gruff and difficult, but have your well-being in mind as his top priority. "Hashem," asked David, "hear the real voice behind my prayer, not just the words, which may be poorly chosen." Rarely does a child who says, "You are the meanest mother in the whole wide world," mean anything more than, "I wish I could stay up a little bit longer than you are permitting me to." Hearing things for what they really are makes life a great deal more manageable.

Outrunning the Blessings

"These blessings will catch up to you, when you listen to the voice of Hashem."[94] This verse is somewhat perplexing; who would run away from a blessing? "Let only goodness and kindness pursue me all the days of my life," asked King David.[95] Why would it need to pursue him; aren't we all engaged in the pursuit of happiness to being with? If it would just stay still, wouldn't that be more than enough?

---

94. *Devarim* 28:2.
95. *Tehillim* 23:6.

The *Degel Machaneh Efraim*[96] explains that all too often, we just have no idea what is best for us. People spend so much time running after things that can't make them happy, nor satisfy them in any way. We all think we know what is best, but it is only God Who really does. King David asked God to continue to make goodness and kindness pursue him; even if we run away from something thinking it's not good for us, even if we beg Hashem to keep that thing away from us, we want Him to ignore those words and have what is really best for us nipping at our heals in pursuit, catching up with us and making us deliriously happy all the days of our lives. The Torah is promising that if you live life in line with what Hashem really wants you to do, then you will, indeed, have blessing, even if you don't know where to look. It will find you.

"Let Hashem hear my voice," we ask. It's not enough to hear our own words sometimes, for we don't always say what we mean, and we don't always know what is best for us.[97] So we beg Hashem to please give us what He knows is best, even if our words sometimes say something else.[98]

Forgetting My Father

In a poignant moment in the life of Joseph, his first beautiful baby boy is born. Inexplicably, he names his son "Menashe,

---

96. *Ki Savo*, s.v. *u-vau*.
97. See R. Avraham ben HaGra in *Be'er Avraham* to *Tehillim* 27:11 p. 31b, *ofen alef* where he speaks of how man does not know what is in his best interest, and only Hashem can guide him to the right place.
98. I subsequently found this interpretation of our verse in *Divrei Moed* (R. David Goldstaff), *Elul*, p. 353.

since Hashem caused me to forget all of my hardship and my father's home."[99] It must have been something special to grow up in the home of Jacob, a man who met angels, who interacted with God, studied Torah with his grandfather Avraham and his father, Isaac. Studying Torah with his father[100] was surely sweeter than any other experience that ever followed that. Why name a child after the devastating fact that he was ripped from such a wonderful family, such a loving father; literally snatched from heaven on earth?[101]

Understanding His Ways

Perhaps the answer is somewhat simple. A person who was sent into the world and encounters obstacles, conditions that seem to be less than ideal, has a problem, for he "knows" that "if only things would be different, then I would be better off." But that is not really so. "Man's steps are from Hashem," said King David,[102] and later, echoed his son Shlomo.[103] Shlomo cites his father's words and adds to them, *va-adam, mah yavin darko*, "What can man understand of His ways?"[104] Joseph realized that man's footsteps are guided by Hashem, and if he finds himself in Egyptian prison rather than in Daddy's warm embrace, then there must be only good in that. He was able to avoid falling into the trap of spending his life quite understandably pining

---

99. *Bereshis* 41:51.
100. See Rashi to *Bereshis* 37:3, s.v. *ben zekunim*, and *Emes le-Yaakov* of R. Yaakov Kamenetsky there.
101. See the powerful answer of R. Kalonymus Kalman Epstein in his *Meor va-Shomesh* to *Bereshis*, ibid.
102. *Tehillim* 37:23.
103. *Mishlei* 20:24.
104. See the important comments of Meiri to *Mishlei* 16:9.

for his father's home, and instead, he celebrated and accepted that this is really Hashem's plan for him, and that his life would be most effectively used in Egypt. This way, he was able to forget for a while about his father's home, and not allow himself to become a bitter person, mourning what was and bemoaning what could have been if only. Having a wonderful Jewish child gave him hope. It gave him a chance to further "forget" his father's home—not entirely, but just enough to move ahead.

Investigation

Va-adam, mah yavin darko? Man really has no way to *yavin darko*, understand His ways. That understanding, or *binah*, is not really something that we are blessed with in advance. We just have to go with the flow. The words *binah* and *Elul* are both numerically equivalent to 67. The word *Elul* means to investigate. The spies that Moshe sent ahead into the land of Israel were told *ve-yasuru*,[105] to "investigate," which is translated by Onkelos as *va-yeallelun*—meaning that they should "Elul" the land out. Elul is a time of investigating. We rethink where we have been, and where we are going. And we also rethink if we truly have known what is best, or if only Hashem does. But becoming aware of our inability to know for certain, we develop a *binah*, an insight into what we really are meant to be doing.

The Vilna Gaon[106] reads this verse somewhat unconventionally: *Va-adam mah? Yavin darko.* "What is man [then to do]? Understand His ways." God sends us many things in life. Our

105. *Bemidbar* 13:2.
106. Commentary to *Mishlei* 20:24, s.v. *me-Hashem.*

role is not to fight them, but to understand the message present in them, and learn how to forget our idealized version of how things could be, and instead, find in our reality a way to make the best contribution, as Joseph did so magnificently in his life.

This is Elul

A century ago, the Tunisian R. Eliyahu HaKohen, in his *Orchos Chaim*,[107] observed that when we take the first letter in the last word of this verse, *va-aneni*, and combine it with the first letters of the next three words that follow it, *lecha amar libbi*, it spells out the word *Elul*.[108] The month of Elul, the month for reciting *Le-Dovid*, is a month where we would do well to make sure that we are not pushing too hard for our version of how life "needs to be." Instead, we should ask Hashem to make sure it works out well, thereby reinforcing in ourselves that though there are times when things don't immediately seem best for us, they may indeed be so. When we discover that we don't know everything and that Hashem really has a much clearer picture of how things ought to be, we will be in a far better place on our paths toward success. Being aware that our words are at times unclear, and that our voices are what need to be heard, is one of the great achievements that can be attained in Elul, and the High Holiday season.

---

107. P. 260, s.v. *shema Hashem koli*.
108. See also *Be'er Avraham* to *Tehillim* 27:7, *ofen beis*, p. 33a, s.v. *shema*, from R. Avraham ben HaGra, citing his father, the Vilna Gaon, that *Shema Hashem koli*, the first words of our verse, refers to Rosh Hashanah, and the following word, *ekra*, refers to Yom Kippur.

8

If You Give a Thirsty Man a Drink!

לְךָ אָמַר לִבִּי בַּקְשׁוּ פָנָי אֶת פָּנֶיךָ ה' אֲבַקֵשׁ :

In your behalf, my heart has said, "Seek My Presence."
Your presence Hashem do I seek.

This verse—*lecha amar libbi bakshu panai es panecha Hashem avakesh*—is likely the hardest one to translate of this Psalm. Above, you see the translation of the ArtScroll Tanach.[109]

Malbim[110] offers another reading: "My heart speaks to You," saying that, "for my face to seek out Your presence, Hashem, is my sincerest request." Nothing else speaks to me the way that this desire does. All that I want is to connect with You and understand You. This is what all my life is about.

---

109. P. 1457. See Rashi *ad loc.*, s.v. *lecha.*
110. To *Tehillim, ad loc.*

What David understood, and we all recite in his footsteps, is that all we want in this life is to be close to Hashem and connected to our true Source.

But first, let's understand a little more what it means to really want something, and how that desire can define us, no matter where we are on the ladder at any given time.

Here I Am!

"You shall come to the *kohen* who will be in those days and you shall say to him, 'I declare today to Hashem, your God, that I have come to the Land that Hashem swore to our forefathers to give us.'"[111] When a person brings his first fruits to the Temple, he is to tell the *kohen* that he has come to the Land. R. Shimon Sofer of Krakow,[112] the son of the *Chasam Sofer*, wonders why there is any need to state this self-evident fact to the *kohen*. After all, the man is standing in Jerusalem—why state the obvious?

He begins his explanation by citing a teaching of his father.[113] The *Chasam Sofer* observes that many times in Rashi's commentary to the Torah,[114] he interprets that when one person is told to "take" another person, it means "persuade that person" and let them be "taken" with your words. He explains that the reason Rashi says this is because it is not really possible to take a person anywhere. A person is made up of spirit, and flesh. The flesh is

---

111. *Devarim* 26:3.
112. *Michtav Sofer, Drush* 1, p. 3, s.v. *amarti*.
113. *Drashos Chasam Sofer* Vol. 2, p. 398b, s.v. *akdim*.
114. E.g., *Vayikra* 8:2, *Bemidbar* 8:6, and more.

not really the main part of a person at all, rather one's mind is. The body is nothing more, says the *Chasam Sofer*, than a "clump of dirt and mud." Thus, taking a person by doing an action to the shell that is their body, without the presence of the mind, could not really be called "taking." You can only take another person by engaging their spirit; their mind and psyche. It is only then that a person moves. R. Shimon Sofer explains as well that this is also how we are to understand Hashem's directive to Avraham,[115] *Lech lecha*, "...to the land that I will show you." According to R. Sofer, *Lech lecha* means, "Go, to you." For Avraham's mind and soul were really in the spiritual place that in the physical plane can be called the Land of Israel. All that he was missing was the bringing of his body there. That was remedied by his "going" with his body "to himself."

R. Yosef Karo wrote almost the same thing: "A man's soul is where his mind is thinking and musing."[116] The Baal Shem Tov also taught, "Wherever a person's mind is, that is where he really is."[117]

Our Sages teach, "There were ten measures of illicit sexual behavior given to the world. Nine of those were taken by the Arabs, and one is for the rest of the world."[118] It is kind of a

---

115. *Bereshis* 12:1.
116. *Magid Meisharim*, Mahadura Kamma, *Beshalach*.
117. Cited in *Toldos Yaakov Yosef* on *Chayei Sarah*, as well as *Degel Machaneh Efraim* (*Shemos*, s.v. *va-ta'al*, as well as *Bereshis*, s.v. *va-yomer*; *Vayera*, s.v. *ve-hu*; and *Masei*, s.v. *ve-od*. The same is taught by R. Tzadok of Lublin. See also *Magid Ta'alumah* to *Brachos* 54a, s.v. *ha-roeh*.
118. *Kiddushin* 49b.

surprising statement. It would certainly appear that the Arab world, for all of their flaws, still has laws about illicit sexual activities, and they take precautions (even if they are the wrong ones) to stop women from dressing immodestly, and to limit such activity. This is far different from the west, where billboards, magazines, and television display all sorts of immoral things, and anything and everything goes. But—nothing can tell you more about a person than hearing about his version of heaven. If a religion teaches that the eternal reward after death is nothing more than a big brothel in the sky, you can know what you need to about that system of living. The Arabs, even should many of them manage to curb their illicit appetites for this world, have given themselves away as people who are living for nothing more than sexuality. "One of the pearls of wisdom[119] that Rav would often repeat was, 'This world is nothing like the World to Come. In the World to Come, there is no eating; no drinking; no physical intimacy; no business is transacted; there is no jealousy, anger, or squabbling; there are only righteous people sitting with their crowns atop their heads, delighting in the glow of the Divine Presence.'"[120] That is Heaven. You are

---

119. The words of the Talmud are, "*margela bifumei*." Rashi (*Brachos* 17a, s.v. *margela*) explains that this more literally means that this was something that he often said. *Yad Rama* (*Sanhedrin* 50b) explains that it also means "a pearl of wisdom."

120. *Brachos* 17a. See R. Isaac Chaver's *Magen Vitzina*, Chap. 25, where he explains that though a person's soul is not limited in its ability to connect with the divine, physical existence severely limits the soul's ability to achieve intellectual and spiritual heights. What a soul can understand in mere moments without a body could never be achieved in even one thousand years while cloaked in physicality. He explains this statement in that light as well. See also the comment of the Vilna Gaon recorded there, that the purpose of sleep is for the soul to be

where your mind is. If every time that you pray, or do a good deed, you believe that this is all about sexuality in the end, then you have truly taken nine of the ten measures of illicit sexual behavior that the world can hold.

R. Shimon Sofer taught that all this is the reason that we have to announce our location. It is a simple matter to physically be located in the Land of Israel. It is a far more challenging matter to be there spiritually. When the fellow says that he has come today to the Land, he is saying, in R. Shimon Sofer's words, "With this brining [of first fruits] with happiness and a good heart, to rejoice before Hashem, to thank Him and bless Him for the desirable good, wide Land that He gave us, with this I announce that I have truly come to the Land." You can only be somewhere when your heart, soul, and mind are there. You are only spending time with your wife and children when your mind is there, and you can truly think to yourself, "I am sitting with my beloved children, and my dear wife, whom I am thankful for." When you can stop your busy life, and make your mind present, you can truly be somewhere. Your body can be locked up, far from the place that you want to be—but you cannot be held back. Nothing can stop your mind from going wherever it needs to. If you ever have to make the choice of being somewhere with either your body or your mind, choose the mind.[121] That is who you really are.

---

able to connect to things that it never could while awake and present in this world.

121. See the very important comments of R. Chaim ben Betzalel, the brother of the Maharal of Prague, in his *Sefer ha-Chaim, Sefer Geulah vi-Yeshuah*, Chap. 1, where he explains that when our Sages taught

Deep Desire

The deepest desire of the Jew is his thirst for Hashem and His mitzvos. As Rashi powerfully says, "Thirsty is [a description of] Israel, who are thirsty and desiring to be in awe of their Creator and fulfill His commandments." [122]

I was once privileged to hear the saintly Rabbi Noah Weinberg describe his meeting with a Torah giant as a young man. At that time, Rabbi Weinberg was seeking counsel about starting a Yeshiva for those who knew nothing about Torah or Judaism. The Rabbi was astounded by the concept, and somewhat skeptical. "What will you do," he asked with a smile, "have a revolving door where people walk in secular and are transformed into Orthodox Jews?" Rabbi Weinberg replied, "If you offer a thirsty man a cup of water, will he turn it down?" To which the great Rabbi replied, "If that is your attitude, I think that you will have great success." Rabbi Weinberg was one of our generation's most successful

---

(*Kesuvos* 110b) that one who lives outside the Land of Israel is like one who worships idols, this is only referring to one who makes his life a life of permanence outside Israel, assimilating into those peoples around him. This is why it says, "One who dwells outside the Land," which implies one's whole mind is set on being there forever. Such an attitude is a denial of God. But one who always hoped for the final redemption and his heart is in the Land of Israel all his life, he is credited as if he were living there all along, and standing there even when distant from the Land itself. This, he explains, is why we must face Jerusalem when praying (*Brachos* 30a, *Shulchan Aruch, Orach Chaim* 94:2), for when we do so, it is literally as if we are standing there. This, he explains, is why Jerusalem is never mentioned in the Torah. It only says (see *Devarim* 12:5), "the place God will chose," for one can connect to God no matter where he finds himself, and be "in Jerusalem" even if he is not physically there.

122. *Sanhedrin* 76b, s.v. *ravah*.

Rabbis in bringing the beauty of Torah to those who might otherwise never have had any exposure to it at all. He was armed with the conviction that the Jewish soul is thirsty for the Torah.

We all want the connection to Hashem. But we certainly don't feel that at all times. This verse tells us, as we all recite it, that what we truly want more than anything else in this life is a deep, dynamic, thriving connection to Hashem, our Creator, and His Torah. Nothing else matters. We must truly strive to be in touch with this, for it is true. We are where our mind and heart are, and our hearts truly want nothing more than to be close to Hashem. If we can know this truly, we will arrive at a connection with Hashem that is so deep, and so immediate.

9

A Nut-Free Environment

אַל תַּסְתֵּר פָּנֶיךָ מִמֶּנִּי אַל תַּט בְּאַף עַבְדֶּךָ עֶזְרָתִי
הָיִיתָ אַל תִּטְּשֵׁנִי וְאַל תַּעַזְבֵנִי אֱ-לֹהֵי יִשְׁעִי :

Do not hide Your presence from me, do not repel Your
servant in anger, You were my Helper, do not abandon me,
do not forsake me, God of my salvation.

Listening to the Heart

Al tat be-af avdecha means, "Do not repel[123] Your servant in
anger." The word *af* means "anger." David asks Hashem to keep
His presence close to him, so that he may not be distanced from
Hashem as a result of *af*. Rabbi Moshe David Walli[124] explains
that "the human heart speaks constantly to a person, letting
him know what has been decreed upon him and how he should

123. See also the approach of R. Avraham ben Ramoch (b. 1360, a
student of the Ran) to *Tehillim* 27:9, who understands it to mean, "Do
not include me among others, even if you are feeling anger toward
them."
124. *Ayin Tikkunim, Tikkun* 69.

react. Even things that a person cannot know, his heart always knows. This is the secret of the most inner part of a person, the part connected to God. [This part of man's psyche] is literally God's messenger to inform and inspire a person for any reason, as it says,[125] 'Though I am sleeping, my heart is awake, the sound of my beloved knocking...."' He explains our verse in this light; King David is asking Hashem not to create any distance between God's presence and his own heart, so that he can have that internal drive to connect to Hashem.[126]

I Still Love You

Af gam zos, "Despite all this," promises Hashem,[127] "while they will be in the land of their enemies, I will not have been revolted by them, nor will I have rejected them, annulling my covenant with them, for I am Hashem, their God!" A child who does something to displease his or her parent is not in any way an enemy of that parent, or hated by them. Even amidst the disappointment of such a parent, the love of a good parent burns strong. It was a seminal moment in my life when I learned this in an experiential way. I came home from shul one morning to discover that my wonderful young daughters had poured a great deal of milk all over the table and floor in a valiant attempt to get enough in each one's cereal bowl for breakfast. As I was expressing displeasure, reminding them to ask for help, and still

---

125. *Shir ha-Shirim* 5:2.
126. He also points out that *libbi*, "my heart," is an acronym of the letters appearing earlier, in verse 4: *la-chazon be-noam Hashem*, meaning that the internal desire to feel true Divine peace and satisfaction is the product of one's heart's connection to Truth and Hashem.
127. *Vayikra* 26:44.

watching these three little girls, each trying to find some sort of towel to mop up the mess, my five-year-old daughter looked up at me and said hopefully , "You still love us *so* much, right?" And then, with more certainty, she asserted, "You just don't want us to make a mess, but you still love us." Hashem loves us so deeply no matter what.

The *Chasam Sofer*[128] explains that when David said, "Do not repel me with *af*," he meant, please do not agree to be with me in the less desirable way of *af gam zos*, "even when they are far, they are indeed near to me." Do not try to appease me with *af*, with, "despite it all, I am with you." That is not enough for us. We desire a direct and compelling relationship with Hashem, nothing short of absolutely ideal.

Stay Away from Nuts!
On Rosh Hashanah, teaches the Rema,[129] there is a custom not to eat nuts (*egozim*), for the numerical value of *egoz*, the Hebrew word for "nut," is the same as that of *chet*, the word for "sin."[130]

---

128. *Drasha* for 27 Elul 5598, printed in *Toras Moshe* to *Parshas Nitzavim* 53a, *Drashos Chasam Sofer* Vol. 2, *Drush* 27, Elul.
129. *Orach Chaim* 583:2.
130. This requires the silent *alef* at the end of *chet* to be left off. See *Degel Machaneh Efraim* (*likkutim Devarim*) citing *Baal Shem Tov*, who explains that the silent *alef* in the world *chet* hints to the fact that one who sins has forgotten Hashem, the *Alef* (Chief) of the world. See also the Midrash *Osiyos de-Rabbi Akiva*: "*Alef, this is G-d.*" The construction of the *alef* is with two *yods* and a *vav*, which equals twenty-six, the numerical value of G-d's four-letter name. For more on this, see the Dinover Rebbe's *Regel Yesharah*, pp. 246, 247. See also Professor Sperber's *Minhagei Yisrael*, Vol. 4, p. 49, for another approach. A final possibility is based upon the idea that *gematria* can still be accurate within one number of the sum, whether one more or one less; this is

In his comments to the *Shulchan Aruch*,[131] the *Chasam Sofer* explains that there is also another reason why we refrain from eating *egozim* on Rosh Hashanah. The verse in *Shir ha-Shrim*[132] calls the Jewish people *egozim*. The Midrash[133] explains, "In what way are the Jewish people similar to the *egoz*? Just as the inside of the *egoz* stays unblemished even when the nut rolls around in filth [due to its protective shell], so the Jewish people have an unblemished inside, no matter how filthy a place they find themselves among the nations of the world." The nut is untouched, only the shell is dirty, and it's what's inside that counts. The *Chasam Sofer* goes on to explain that since the

referred to as *im ha-kollel*. This is found in *Bemidbar Rabbah* 18:21, which equates *yirah* and *Torah*. See *Baal ha-Turim* to *Bereshis* 48:5; *Midrash Talpios* (*Anaf Emes*, s.v. *Efraim*), who elaborates on this, explaining that "a difference of one just doesn't matter." See also Chida in his *Devash Lifi* (*Gimmel*, 14), citing *Likkutei Gurei ha-Ari*, and *Rema [mi-Fano] Kesav Yad* (cited in *Bnei Yissaschar*, Sivan 2:13, and Kislev Teves 2:2–3). See *Leket Yosher* (intro, s.v. *ve-karasi*), who quotes the *Terumas ha-Deshen* as bringing a proof to this idea from *Gittin* 88a, and Rashi there (s.v. *Ulla*). See also *Birkas Peretz* in his introduction to the *parperaos*. In his weekly Torah essay, on *Vayakhel*, R. Yaakov Hillel cites R. Yehuda Koriat, author of *Meor va-Shemesh*, who explains that when a *gematria* is done with the *kollel*, it is adding to it the awareness that something complete is more than just the sum of its parts, and is instead a new being, a step above merely its individual components. He explains that this is why one is sometimes added to the numerical value. See also the comments of R. Yosef Engel, in his *Beis ha-Otzar* (Vol. 1, *klal* 48, s.v. *echad*, and s.v. *ve-od ayin*), where he proves that being one short is never considered *chisaron* (lacking) in many, many arenas. He uses this to explain *gematria* being off by one, among many other absolutely fascinating postulations. It's worth looking up. See also his *Asvin de-Oraysa, klal* 22, s.v. *ve-hinnei.*

131. *Hagahos Chasam Sofer* to *Shulchan Aruch, Orach Chaim* 583, s.v. *she-egoz.*

132. 6:11.

133. *Shir ha-Shirim Rabbah* 6:17.

egoz reminds us of those nations who sully our experience, at least externally, in this life, it's not the right message for Rosh Hashanah, where everything we eat is laden with symbolism. Furthermore, he adds that *egoz* is an acronym for the first letters of the three words, *af gam zos*, the verse we mentioned earlier, where Hashem says, "Despite it all, I will be with you."

No Compromise

The saintly Rabbi Yissachar Teichtel, may Hashem avenge his blood, wondered about the reasoning behind this teaching of the *Chasam Sofer*.[134] Isn't this the perfect thing to pray for on the High Holidays, that we be protected by Hashem from those who want to harm us, that even when we find ourselves in impossible situations where He appears to be absent, that we still should be capable of knowing His presence? No, he explains, we don't want that second-rate sort of relationship.[135] He quotes the earlier words of the *Chasam Sofer*, explaining King David's plea. We want Hashem not to have to watch us kicked around like the *egoz* through the mud, and know that deep down inside, we are untouched, and our connection is solid. As important as that feeling is for times of trouble, our prayers for the new year are that it be one of salvation, light, clarity, and perfection. That it be a year where things go right.

No couple starts their marriage with hopes that the coming year will bring them rocky paths and horrible tribulations where

---

134. *Mishneh Sachir, Moadim* Vol. 1, *Yamim Noraim*, p. 193.
135. See also the relevant comments of R. Azariah Figo (author of *Binah le-Ittim*) in his *Chevel Naim* to *Tehllim* 27:4, s.v. *achas shaalti*.

through the worst of it, their therapy can help them cope and know of a deep but hidden love. That's not at all what we are setting out to build in our relationship with Hashem either. While we know that things are unbreakable, we'd rather not test that out at all. Our relationship with Hashem, as we envision it on Rosh Hashanah, is to be a nut-free environment, free of *egoz* and free of *af*.[136] We dream big, for we do have hopes of getting it right this time around. Our big plans, our Rosh Hashanahs, need to be complete plans—not plans to survive or just make it, but to thrive. Let's make this year the year where we get it right, without a nut in sight.[137]

---

136. See also the enlightening comments of R. Eliezer HaLevi Horowitz in his *Amaros Tehoros* to *Tehillim* 27:9, where he explains that the verse (*Mishlei* 21:14) explains that charity overcomes God's anger, His *af*. But, the *Gemara* in *Bava Basra* (6a) explains that this is because we are called Hashem's children. Since our Sages tell us (see *Bava Basra* 10a) that if we are not doing the will of Hashem, we are no longer like children, but like servants. In such a situation, we would then be unable to avoid His *af*.

137. It is interesting to note that some continue to avoid eating nuts all the way until the end of the holiday season, through Hoshanah Rabbah; for just the same length of time that we recite *Le-Dovid*. See *Piskei Teshuvos* to *Or ha-Chaim*, ibid., who quotes sources in this vein.

10

The Abandoned Baby

כִּי אָבִי וְאִמִּי עֲזָבוּנִי וַה׳ יַאַסְפֵנִי:

When my father and mother abandoned me,
Hashem gathered me in.

Free of Sin

King David had an exceptional father. He was so righteous and free of sin that if not for Eve having been enticed by the serpent in Eden, he never would have died. Most people sin at least once, and if one sins, death is the result.[138] "There were four people who died only because [Eve accepted] the advice of the serpent," teaches the Talmud,[139] and one of those four was Yishai, King David's father. He was completely free of sin, and only died because all of mankind was punished with death after the sin of Adam and Eve.

---

138. *Shabbos* 55a.
139. *Shabbos* 55b.

"King David said," records the Midrash,[140] "Did Father Yishai intend to bring me to this world, why he was only seeking his own enjoyment. This is indeed the case, for as soon as my parents satisfied their needs, this one turned his head to one side, and the other turned her head to the other side, but You, Hashem, gather in each and every drop, and this is what King David said, 'When my father and mother abandoned me, Hashem gathered me in.'"

It is surprising to hear that Yishai, a fellow who never ever sinned, exhibited such behavior, seeking his own pleasure. After all, the highest level, we are taught,[141] is that a person's intention in marital intimacy is not meant to be just for personal pleasure, but instead in order to fulfill a holy obligation, a mitzvah, to bring children to this world.[142] It is interesting to consider, then, that Yishai, such a refined person, is described and recorded in *Tehillim* as having been almost disinterested in having children, and seeking only his own pleasure.

Spiritual Venom

R. Tzadok of Lublin[143] explains that "taking the advice of the serpent," which is what brought death to all people, actually means that all people are infected with a bit of the serpent's spiritual venom, which he calls *shoresh ha-taavah*, "the root of

---

140. *Vayikra Rabbah* 14:5.
141. See, for example, *Tur, Orach Chaim* 231.
142. See *Tur*, ibid., where this is listed as one of the appropriate focuses. See also Rambam, *Issurei Biah* 21:9: "For this whole activity is really all about being fruitful and multiplying."
143. *Tzidkas ha-Tzaddik* 257.

desire." He illustrates this with the above teaching about Yishai, that even he was motivated by his own desire. In other words, even the finest of people are still human, and motivated by their own desires a little bit. It is to cleanse this connection to the physical desire that we are all destined to die. Thus the Talmud was teaching that there were some people who were as free from sin as possible, but even they could not be completely free of desire and were incapable of being completely altruistic with nothing at all personally involved. There is a part of man that always remains unrefined.

No Blessing Can Be Made...

Though we make blessings on so many physically pleasurable activities, like eating and drinking, smelling pleasant smells, seeing beautiful things, and hearing awe-inspiring natural sounds, we do not make a blessing on marital intimacy.[144] The *Noam Elimelech*[145] explains that this is because the experience of marital intimacy cannot be without some element of personal desire, and cannot be done exclusively and entirely for the mitzvah alone. Therefore, no blessing was established by our sages for this pleasure. R. Zvi Hirsch of Ziditchov[146] elaborates

---

144. See Maharsha to *Brachos* 57b, s.v. *shloshah ain*, that one only makes a blessing on something that enters the body. Rav Yosef Chaim of Baghdad has the same approach in his *Rav Paalim* Vol. 3, *Orach Chaim* 10.

145. *Vayishlach*, s.v. *o yirtzeh va-ye'avek*, citing "*poskim*." Note the observation of his great-nephew the Dinover Rebbe (the *Bnei Yissaschar*) in his *Derech Pikudecha* (Mitzvah 1, *Chelek ha-Dibbur* 6), that he never found any such thing in any of the *poskim*, and his acknowledgement that "my not having seen it proves nothing."

146. Cited by his *mechutan* in *Derech Pikudecha* (ibid., 5).

in the name of the Chozeh of Lublin, that even the best of people cannot be perfectly focused on just spirituality during intimacy, proving this from what we know about Yishai.[147]

David's Beginnings

According to one rabbinic source, there was even more going on when King David was conceived. *Yalkut ha-Machiri*,[148] a collection of Midrashim, tells us of King David's conception. Yishai was planning to marry his maidservant.[149] But his wife slipped into the bed, and not realizing this, he impregnated her with King David. To his knowledge, however, he had only been with his maidservant, and not his wife. The family presumed David to be an illegitimate child, until Shmuel the prophet came and chose him as the king.[150]

King David recognizes that all of us, no matter how righteous his or her parents may have been, still come from an act motivated

---

147. See more on this in the Dinover Rebbe's *Agra de-Pirka* 197, as well as his *Hosafos* to the Ziditchover's *Sur me-Ra va-Asei Tov* (*os* 44), and R. Yaakov Emden's *Mor u-Ketziyah* 240. Regarding the absence of a blessing on *biah rishonah*, see *Sifsei Kohen al ha-Torah* (*Metzora*, s.v. *vee ki seitzei*), and *Mor u-Ketziyah* 640, s.v. *li-shoel*.
148. On *Tehillim* 118:28. See *Alfa Beisa Kadmisa di-Shmuel Zeira*, p. 239. See also Rabbi Dovid Cohen's *Ohel Dovid*, Vol. 2, p. 83-84 to *Tehillim* 27:10 where he explains our verse in light of this Midrash.
149. Rema Mi-Fano (*Asarah Maamaros, Maamar Chikur Din* 3:10) explains that this was because the law about a Jew marrying a person of Moabite descent was not yet perfectly clear in his time, and thus, he was separating from his wife for the time being, since he was a descendant of Ruth.
150. For more on this absolutely fascinating topic, see my *Paradise: Breathtaking Strolls through the Length and Breadth of Torah* (Urim, 2012) to *Parashas Mattos*.

by a degree of selfishness; a bit of non-altruism. And yet even in that place of imperfection, God is right there to gather one in, and build a person despite anyone else's motivations.

Abandoned and Found

Perhaps there is even another level to this. King David, the ancestor of Moshiach ben David, for whom we long, is the beginning of a dynasty that teaches us how to perfect the world in which we live. It is not despite our human and selfish side that we can be great, but precisely because we were built that way that our achievements are worthwhile. It is the selfishness and the *yetzer hara* with which we can make the greatest dent in this life. Moshiach, who brings the world to a state of perfection, is the one who teaches *teshuvah*, just as King David himself taught us to repent, after his incident with Batsheva. [151] The serpent, who infects us all, is in Hebrew called a *nachash*, whose numerical value of three hundred fifty-eight is identical to the numerical value of *moshiach*,[152] for our salvation is defined by

151. *Avodah Zarah* 5a.
152. *Tosafos ha-Shalem* to *Shemos* 7:15, 2, R. Chaim Vital in *Sefer ha-Likkutim* to *Yeshaya* 38, *Sifsei Kohen al ha-Torah* to *Shemos* 30:34, Ramchal in *Adir ba-Marom* p. 338 and *Kinas Hashem Tzivaos* in *Ginzei Ramchal* p. 89, R. Moshe Dovid Walli, *Sefer ha-Hanhagah* to *Koheles* 10:8 and his commentary to *Mishlei* 12:25 (p. 155), *Zecher Dovid* (Modina) *Maamari Shlishi, limmud leil Shavuos* p. 281 in Ahavat Shalom ed., *Chida in Midbar Kedemos, dalet* 19, *Bnei Yissaschar, maamrei chodesh Marcheshvan,* 1:2, and *maamarei Kislev-Teves* 2:25, *Regel Yesharah mem* 124, *Likkutei Mahartza* to *Bereshis,* s.v. *yishretzu, Lechem le-Fi ha-Taf (shin* 13). See also *Dan Yadin* 14 cited in the *Regel Yesharah* ibid., *Chesed Le-Avraham, maayan* 4, 58, *Shaar ha-Kavanos, Drushei Pesach* 14, *Taamei ha-Mitzvos* to *Tetzaveh,* and *Lechem min ha-Shomayim of Chida* to *Tetzaveh* 11. See also *Tzidkas ha-Tzaddik* 157, *Dover Tzedek* 2, *Yisrael Kedoshim* 5, all of R. Tzadok Hakohen of Lublin.

how we handle the parts of us that are as yet incomplete. What do we do with the places in our life where God appears to be absent; what do we do when feeling uninspired, disconnected. King David taught us that in that very space where one could be abandoned by even his parents, Hashem is still there. There is no space without Hashem.

Great Orphans

Great saviors of the Jewish people were often those who were dislodged from the comfort of their families in serious ways.[153] David was "abandoned by his parents," and even shunned by them. Moshe, the first great redeemer of the Jews, was not raised by his own parents. Yiftach was disowned by his family.[154] The great Queen Esther was an orphan, her father having died after conception, and her mother, in childbirth.[155] And in her finest moment, she risked everything to save the Jewish people, going willfully to Achashverosh, a move that would render her unable, according to Jewish law, to ever return to Mordechai.[156] Mordechai was her whole world. He was her adoptive father, her husband, her everything. "Just as I lost my father and mother, I will be lost from you too!"[157] Until that point, she had been a victim of coercion and could have returned to Mordechai

---

153. See *Divrei Yechezkel* to *Brachos* 48a, where he discusses the unique relationship of orphans to Hashem, and how the great Abaye, himself and orphan, expressed that as a youngster.
154. *Shoftim*, chap. 11.
155. *Megillah* 13a. See *Yaaros Devash* Vol. 2, *Drush* 2, for an elaboration upon why it had to be so with Esther, who was combating Amalek, the descendant of Esav who excelled in his honoring his father.
156. *Megillah* 15a.
157. *Megillah* ibid.

eventually. In one of the most heartbreaking decisions that anyone in Scripture ever makes, she plunged herself into a lonely world where Hashem was to be her only ally.

A person who can find Hashem in the places where he would otherwise have been abandoned, without anything, is a person of greatness. We all have that place where we are battling alone, where nobody can help us. But Hashem is there. Our relationship with Hashem, as we make Him our King, is that of our dearest, closest, most beloved friend. The One Who is there even when nobody else is.

11

Springs, Pits, and Life

הוֹרֵנִי ה׳ דַּרְכֶּךָ וּנְחֵנִי בְּאֹרַח מִישׁוֹר לְמַעַן שׁוֹרְרָי׃

*Teach me Your way, Hashem, and lead my on the path
of integrity because of those who watch me.*

People Are Watching

King David asks to be led down the path of integrity because
of "*shorerai*," those who are watching him. Most[158] understand
this to mean his watchful enemies, who were just waiting for his
downfall.

Rabbi Shlomo Kluger[159] explains that there are always people
who follow the life of the *tzaddik* and consider his behavior. If
they find the *tzaddik* behaving in a pleasant and agreeable way,
this influences their behavior, but if they see that he does not

---

158. For example, see Rashi to *Tehillim* 5:9, s.v. *shorerai*, Ibn Ezra
there, and *Metzudos* there and here.
159. *Tehillos Yisrael* 27:11, s.v. *horeini*, p. 426.

follow the path of integrity, then they conclude that service of God is worthless[160] and the mitzvos are for naught. King David was motivated to beseech Hashem for assistance in making the right choices, in picking the side of integrity, so that those who would be watching him would see clearly the difference between a person of Torah and a person not influenced by it.

When a person enters the *beis midrash* to study Torah, he should say, "May it be Your will, Hashem, my God, that no mistake come through me, that I not err in a matter of *halachah*, and then my friends will be happy as a result of me...."[161] Rashi[162] explains that one is meant to ask that nobody find pleasure in his mistakes, thereby causing not only a mistake, but also the unfortunate result of the friends being punished for their unwarranted joy. Rabbi Moshe Chaim Litch-Rosenbaum, in his *Lechem Rav*,[163] offers another interpretation. A person is meant to be worried lest he suggest something in the course of his learning that sounds brilliant and on the mark, in case it seems so compelling that those learning with him do not catch the flaw, and instead rejoice in it. Firstly, one does not want to make a mistake, but if he does, he asks Hashem that it at least not capture the fancy of his friends. For then, they will be under the mistaken influence of a false Torah teaching. And so, the Rav explains, King David asked of Hashem: Please allow me to

---

160. See Malachi 3:14.

161. *Brachos* 28b.

162. *Ad loc.*

163. *Lechem Rav ha-Shalem*, p. 476, in Jerusalem 1984 ed. First printed in Kleinvardin, 1921.

know "Your ways," but not only that, please help me know how to implement them along "the path of integrity," on the playing field of life and implementation. This is most important, he concludes, "because of those who watch me." The people who look to King David as a spiritual leader and guide need to see a proper example of how to live, and if he were to be giving them a poor example, then that would have a very negative impact on so many people![164]

Springs and Pits

Everything that we do in this life is meant to be for a purpose. We are given life so that we can produce and give. A spring that produces water of its own is called a *be'er* in Hebrew, and the water that comes from it is called *mayim chaim*, living water. A *bor*, on the other hand, is a pit, or cistern, into which rainwater collects. It holds whatever water is put into it, but it does not have a source of its own for water, and can never add any water to our supply. It is just a receptacle. The *Shev Shma'atsa*[165] explains that life is all about earning and producing. Before a soul is sent down to this world, it is missing nothing, connected to God, and happy. It was sent here in order to not just receive goodness as a gift, he explains, but rather to earn it. So *chaim*, the word for "life," is appropriately the same term for a spring producing its own water, for what life is all about is earning one's keep, and producing one's own water.

---

164. A very similar approach can be found in *Yalkut Eliezer* to *Tehillim* 26:12, s.v. *ragli*, at the very end.
165. Introduction.

Sonei mattanos yichyeh, "One who despises gifts will surely live," said Shlomo.[166] If one abhors taking, and embraces giving, he will surely "live." A poor man, our Sages inform us,[167] is suffering a fate that makes his life almost like death. For one who cannot give is missing out on so much life. And, he explains, this is the depth behind the teaching of our Sages[168] that wicked people are essentially considered dead even while they are living, whereas the righteous live on long after their death. The wicked drain the earth of resources and offer nothing in return. The righteous produce and give to such a degree that the contributions they make benefit the world long after they have departed.

Living for Others

When a person learns that life is about what you give and produce, rather than what you consume, he has indeed gotten to the heart of what Torah living is about. One of the greatest methods of making this life worthwhile is to become the sort of person that other people need around, explains Rabbi Yisrael Salanter.[169] If the lives of others are improved by what we are doing, then we can be certain that we are justifying our existence, explained Rabbi Salanter.[170] The most effective way to

---

166. *Mishlei* 15:27; see also *Kiddushin* 59a.
167. *Nedarim* 64b.
168. *Brachos* 18b. See also *Siddur Yaavetz, Maamados le-Yom Rishon*, for another explanation, and *Yismach Moshe* to *Beshalach* for another approach. See also R. Chaim Palagi in his *Shaalos u-Teshuvos Lev Chaim* (Vol. 2, 6), where he opines that just as one who touches a dead body must wash his hands, so must one who touches a wicked person, for they are considered truly dead even while alive. See also my *Birchasa ve-Shirasa* to *Brachos, ad loc.*, s.v. *eilu.*
169. Cited by Rabbi Dessler in his *Michtav me-Eliyahu*, Vol. 4, p. 269.
170. Cited in *Daas Chochmah u-Musar*, Vol. 2, p. 288. See also *Alei Shur*, Vol. 2, p. 419.

make sure that we can be deemed worthy of being given more time to accomplish in this life is when we can be certain to live for others, and improve their lives.

With this in mind, we can truly understand why King David mentioned those watching him. It's crucial that our impact on the world be a positive one. During Elul, as we consider our place in the grand scheme of humanity, with God as Creator and King, and we plot out our coming year, we recite *Le-Dovid*, and we learn, from this verse, that people are watching. The world is filled with many others. We are not alone; we cannot forget that—for only by offering our waters to others do we really, truly live.

12

Principles of Persuasion

אַל תִּתְּנֵנִי בְּנֶפֶשׁ צָרָי כִּי קָמוּ בִי עֵדֵי שֶׁקֶר וִיפֵחַ חָמָס :

Do not deliver me up to the will of my foes, for false
witnesses have risen up against me and one who
sanctimoniously does wrong.

Becoming What They Wish

R. Hirsch[171] explains, "Do not deliver me up to my foes. Do not
let me become the person that they wish me to be. Let me not
be that which they slanderously claim that I am. False witnesses
have risen against me. There is one man, in particular, who while
he does not openly accuse me of wrongdoing, hypocritically
and sanctimoniously insinuates it. Such veiled slander is even
more *chamas* than openly voiced accusations, because it robs
me of my good repute."[172]

---

171. Commentary to *Tehillim* 27:12.
172. On this point, it is worthwhile to cite from Rav Hirsch's "Open
Response" to the Wurzburger Rav, Rabbi Seligmann Baer Bamberger
of May 13, 1877 (*Collected Writings*, Vol. 6 p. 256-7) where he

"Let me not be that which they slanderously claim that I am." At first glance, this sort of a request seems a bit strange. What possible danger is there in a person living up to his slanderers after the fact? If someone spreads rumors about you that you robbed a bank, is there now any more danger of your going out and doing so?

Influences

We are all aware of the influence that prevalent beliefs and norms have on our own personal ways of thinking. The

---

writes, "You launch a campaign against me which the thoughtful conscientious Rabbi Bamberger of an earlier day would surely never have committed. You say that you could have a great deal to say against me but refrain from doing so in order not to violate the prohibition of *malbin pnei chavero be-rabbim,* humiliating another person in public, a prohibition, you realize 'in all its momentous and shocking significance.' However, you fail to see that, precisely by stating that you seek to guard against this sin, it is already being committed to the greatest possible extent, 'in all its shocking significance.' If someone would publicly call me a thief, a murderer, and ignoramus, or an idiot, he would certainly have dealt me a grievous insult. But such insults have only a limited effect; they do not transcend the spoken word. However one who publicly says to me that he could have said a great deal more against me if he were not afraid to commit the sin of humiliating another person in public in all its momentous and shocking significance—well dear Sir, such a person has attacked me with the most serious libel possible. For he has left to the imagination of the public a limitless assortment of outrages which, were they made public, could undermine my personal honor. This is so clear and obvious that any schoolboy would readily understand it. To take the liberty of transgressing a prohibition in the greatest measure possible at the very moment when one cites sources from *Mishnah Avos, Gemara Bava Metzia,* Rambam, reminding oneself of the momentous significance of such a transgression, to be cavalierly and thoughtlessly permissive for oneself when as a scholar one should rather be stringent on oneself and lenient for others, demonstrates that at that moment he is not even fit to hand down a ruling."

Rambam teaches,[173] "It is the way that humans were created, to be influenced in their attitudes and actions by friends and colleagues, behaving like others in their land. Therefore a person must attach to righteous people and sit among the wise at all times, in order to learn from their ways, and must avoid wicked people stumbling through the darkness so as to avoid picking up their ways." He goes on to explain that it would be obligatory to move to a desert all alone if that were the only place to avoid wicked people. It is crucial to note that the Rambam never suggests anything akin to "being strong, and knowing who you are inside." Just as someone who is worried about getting burnt by the sun's rays cannot just "be strong" in his belief that his skin will remain unburned, and instead must cover up or stay out of direct sunlight; so must a person be vigilant about the negative influence of others. We were created this way. The only possible solution is to be around the right emotional and spiritual influences, and avoid dangerous ones.

Jewish Day Schools

This is a very important principle when choosing communities to live in, places to pray, and schools for our children. Teachers can teach, and educators can develop curricula, but the power of the social influence of friends and the dominating culture in their social circles is the most powerful influence of all. One of the greatest values of Torah day schools is the great benefit of sending our children to be around other children who come from homes of Torah values. When studying in a fine Yeshiva

---

173. *De'os* 6:7.

on the East Coast, a fellow student and I were once eating in someone's home for a Shabbos meal, and the host continued to make poor jokes throughout the meal. My friend was laughing as if he was hearing the funniest things of his life. After the meal, he turned to me, once we were down the block, and said to me, "I don't know what's wrong with you; when someone is trying to get you to laugh, it doesn't matter how terrible the joke is, you have got to laugh." That comment hit home in a way that no lecture from a great Rabbi could have. It is in order to find our children friends like these, from homes that taught values and consideration and Torah, that we send them to the right schools. No matter the price, it's a bargain.

We understand that our beliefs can change when others think differently. We just start, almost by osmosis, to think like others around us. This is the teaching of the Rambam. But can telling someone what they can or cannot become have an impact on them?

How to Know If You Are Going to Die

"Rabbi Ami taught," says the Talmud,[174] "if one wants to know if they will survive the year or not, they can take a candle during the ten days between Rosh Hashanah and Yom Kippur and place it in a home where there is no draft; if the light continues to burn, one can know that he will live. One who wants to do a business transaction, but is uncertain if this endeavor will succeed or not, can raise a rooster; if it grows fat and attractive,

---

174. *Kreisos* 5b.

he can know that he will succeed. If one is going to embark on a journey, and he wants to know if he will ever make it home, he can enter a dim house; if he can make out his reflection, then he can know that he will make it home. But one should not try this, for perhaps one will feel agonizingly helpless, and his *mazel* will then go bad. Abaye said, now that we know that *simanim* [symbols] are indeed something, on Rosh Hashanah a person should be sure to eat gourd, clover, leeks, beets, and dates."

This teaching of the Talmud is deeply perplexing. The reason not to use these methods of predicting the future, it says, is because perhaps one could get a poor result, indicating that one is going to die, and thereby become so distressed that it indeed comes true. So, do these signs accurately foretell the future or not? If the sign said that the man was going to die, then what does his subsequent depression upon learning that "fact" have to do with him dying? It was already in the cards! We see from here that there is, indeed, a huge power within our minds to become what we are told we will become. If we are told that we are going to die, that is extremely dangerous. The real power of *simanim*, concludes the Talmud, is not to find out what is going to happen, but to influence what is going to happen. And so, says Abaye, this is the absolutely perfect way to begin our yearly journey. We need to take control of what we think our year should look like, and so we do all kinds of *simanim*.

You Can Never…

Who knows the power of telling a young child, "You can never be a doctor." The power of having someone believe in you is immeasurably great. And similarly, when we tell a person who they are or what they are to become, there is a great deal of influence there. This can be used very positively. When one child is just raising his hand to hit another child in frustration, and a teacher or parent says to him, "I can see you are upset. And I am very proud that you are not hitting your brother," most of the time, the child will lower his or her hand. When we tell someone not only that they are good, but what positive things we anticipate from them, and how great they are expected to become, it has a powerful impact. But it can also be used very negatively; people can impress upon others to behave and live in ways that are not true to their nature. People can make choices of professions that are not something that they really want because they were led to believe, from the earliest ages, that "you can never be a doctor; you aren't smart like your sister."

When someone is being told who and what they can and cannot become, when they are being informed what is possible and what is just not possible, it is very hard to break free from that.

The Very First Time: Record Setters

R. Shlomo Ganzfried[175] asks why it is that *Akeidas Yitzchak* is considered by the Torah to be a test for Avraham rather than Yitzchak. "And Hashem tested Avraham."[176] Wasn't Yitzchak's

---

175. *Apiryon* to *Bereishis* 22:1.
176. *Bereishis* 22:1.

giving up of his life a great challenge as well? He quotes the *Drashos ha-Ran*, who explains that after the very first time in world history that a challenge is overcome, that challenge becomes far easier for everyone else to overcome, themselves. Avraham, he explains, had already offered his life up for Hashem when Nimrod attempted to kill him in the fiery furnace of Ur Kasdim. It was thus not as great a challenge for his son Yitzchak to give his life for Hashem. But to give one's child had never been done. Thus, Avraham was the only one legitimately challenged to the ultimate degree, for he was told to do something that had never, ever been done before.

It has always intrigued me how, when world records that have stood for years are broken, they sometimes are then broken many times over in quick succession. Roger Bannister's four-minute mile, or Roger Maris' long-standing home-run record are just two examples. Just after they were broken, there came a succession of people who broke those same records again, and quickly! After one person does something, it is somehow much easier for others to follow suit. This also offers us deep insight into what our forefathers have done for us. For a Jew today to sacrifice for Hashem, for Shabbos, for kosher food—all these tests have been successfully passed before—and thus, we can and must know that it is within our reach to pass these tests as well. We are privileged to come from such giants.[177]

---

177. See my *Paradise: Breathtaking Strolls through the Length and Breadth of Torah* (Urim, 2012) to *Nitzavim* for more on this topic.

David was concerned lest he become what people were defining him to be. As long as people control our sense of what is possible, and what should be, and who we are destined to be, we are doomed to capitulate to them. But we need not be. We can be trendsetters, and break from the mold, if we have confidence that they are wrong, and we shield ourselves from their barbs and taunts, and listen to the voice of Hashem, and the righteous among us.

As we kick off our year, we must make sure that our days between Rosh Hashanah and Yom Kippur are filled with vision that can portend achievement and life. For then, we will conceive of great things, and our *mazel* can thrive.

13

Money, Elul, and Being Wistful!

לוּלֵא הֶאֱמַנְתִּי לִרְאוֹת בְּטוּב ה' בְּאֶרֶץ חַיִּים:

Had I not trusted that I would see the goodness
of Hashem in the land of life!

King David looks back and acknowledges that his enemies
(mentioned in the verse above) would have gotten the best of
him, had he not had confidence in the goodness of Hashem,
explains Rashi.[178]

Lulei Spells Elul

R. Chaim Palagi[179] teaches us that *lulei*, the Hebrew word that
translates as "had I not," is made up of the same four letters as
the word *Elul*, the month of repentance in which we customarily
recite this chapter of *Tehillim*, in which this term appears, twice

---

178. 27:13, s.v. *lulei*.
179. *Nefesh Chaim, Alef* 76, s.v. *Elul*, citing *Eretz ha-Chaim*. See also R.
Avraham Palagi's *Va-Yashkem Avraham* to *Tehillim* 27:13.

daily. One has to wonder what King David's sentiments in this verse have to do with the month of repentance. King David looks back here on what he did right in the past, and realizes how good it was for him. *Teshuvah* would seem to be the very opposite idea; one reflects upon his or her mistakes with regret, and pledges not to make those mistakes again.[180] What role does looking back on one's achievements play in a successful Elul?

Happy!

"Who is wealthy?" wonder our Sages.[181] "The person happy with what he has," they answer. Wealth is so relative. The amenities enjoyed by the poorest person in our society today are far more elaborate and luxurious than the wealthiest person could have imagined several hundred years ago. Happiness, we learn, is not a function of how much one has, but rather of how little one misses. This lesson would seem to apply clearly to the material arena, but should one feel satisfied with his spiritual achievements as well? At first, one might think that this could breed complacency—after all, is the growing person not always striving to reach even higher rungs on the ladder of growth?

It was much to my surprise when I first came across sources that encouraged one to "be happy with what he has," even in matters of spirituality. But indeed, R. Shmuel de Uzida[182] and the Vilna Gaon[183] both said this![184]

---

180. Rambam, *Teshuvah* 2:2.
181. *Avos* 4:1.
182. *Midrash Shmuel* to *Avos, ad loc.,* s.v. *perush ha-sheni.*
183. *Menuchah u-Kedushah* of R. Yisrael Isserel of Ponovezh, the son of R. Dov Ber of Vilna, *Shaar ha-Torah, chelek* 2, 23.
184. See also the similar remarks of *Sfas Emes* to *Avos, ad loc.* See also

Slow Down

Indeed, the great Rabbi Yosef Chaim of Baghdad, as a young man, wrote a letter to Rabbi Eliyahu Mani, the Rabbi of Chevron, which included a question that appeared to be about kabbalistic practice. In one of his responsa,[185] he cites from the letter that he received back from this great sage, who discouraged him from embarking upon such a kabbalistic endeavor at this stage, and cited the work *Pri ha-Aretz* that when our Sages tell us to be happy with what we have, they are referring to our spiritual lot. This is an important idea; one must not jump too quickly in his observance,[186] but instead grow in a measured and unrushed way. After all, if one tries to skip too many rungs while climbing the ladder, he can land at the bottom, losing all of his progress in one fell swoop.[187] The *Eshel Avraham* of Butchatch in his

---

R. Chaim Palagi's *Amudei Chaim* (*Amud ha-Torah* 20) regarding why the Torah was not given in the Land of Israel. The sixth of his nineteen answers is that in the Land of Israel, the Jewish people would have been required to observe many more mitzvos, since there are many more that must be observed only in the Land of Israel, and this would simply be too much for them to do, since the method of bringing people close to Torah can be learned from the way that we teach a convert only some of the simple and some of the hard mitzvos, but not more so that we do not alienate him by the sheer size of the Torah (*Yevamos* 47a; see Rambam, *Issurei Biah* 14:2).

185. *Rav Pealim*, Vol. 3, *Sod Yesharim* 13.

186. *Chasam Sofer* (*Toras Moshe, Acharon shel Pesach*, s.v. *shmor es chodesh*) cites his Rebbe, R. Pinchas HaLevi Horowitz, as teaching this very idea. See R. Pinchas HaLevi Horowitz on this topic in his *Panim Yafos* on the Torah (*Haazinu*, s.v. *ke-nesher yair*). See also the *Ohev Yisrael* (*Likkutim Chadashim, Vayikra*) on the topic of "*likol dibur kadma kriya*." See more on this topic in my *Birchasa ve-Shirasa* to *Brachos* 43b, s.v. *psiyah gassah*.

187. Vilna Gaon to *Mishlei* 19:2 (s.v. *gam be-lo daas*) says clearly that one should grow step by step in his character growth, and compares it to climbing a ladder, where skipping a rung can cause a fall. See

Siddur Tefillah le-Dovid,[188] commenting on the line from the Shabbos song that goes, "*hiluchach tihei be-nachas, oneg kara la-Shabbos*," which means, "Your method of walking should be relaxed, Shabbos is called a delight," explains it along these lines. He explains that the truly righteous person does nothing extreme, but instead grows steadily, enjoys the delights of

---

also his comments to 13:25, about not learning too quickly, since it will not remain with a person. On this topic, it is worthwhile to cite some important sources about learning slowly with a focus on developing one's level of learning rather than focusing on rushing through material. In the introduction to the 5692 Warsaw edition of *Chiddushei Rabbi Akiva Eiger* to *Chullin*, R. Naftali Silverberg wrote, "I must inform you of what I heard from my teacher R. Yaakov Simcha Rafish [the *Shaarei Simchah*]: that his teacher Rabbi Akiva Eiger would instruct his superb students and the students of his students, who were formidable Rabbis themselves, that the primary focus of learning, and toiling at it, should be to develop one's intellect, even if this will compromise the amount of material that one will cover, since there is never enough time. For one whose intellect is truly sharp will avoid wild conclusions that contradict the Talmud, Tosafos and Ramban, etc., for everything they wrote is the pinnacle of straight thinking and concluding the opposite of them is the essence of perverse thinking, and one who has a clear mind will be saved from the pitfall of these mistakes, may God save us from those conclusions." See R. Chaim of Volozhin's letter to his grandson (printed in the *U-Vacharta ba-Chaim* edition of *Ruach Chaim on Avos*, p. 269), where he writes (on p. 270), "The main thing is to grasp on to *svarah ha-yesharah* [accurate way of thinking], and that which is not exactly accurate or clearly refined should be avoided. When one looks carefully, one will notice that the greatest of the *Rishonim* were never praised for anything but their sharp and accurate methods of thinking; whoever was considered more sharp in his way of thinking was considered greater than his companions as a result." In the *U-Vacharta ba-Chaim* commentary there, he cites the book *Meorei ha-Moadim* (Shavuos) that someone asked Rabbi M. Dovid Soloveitchik, *shlita*, about this letter of R. Chaim Volozhin's, based upon *Horayos* 14a, "*ha-kol tzrichin le-marei chitaya*." See there for more on this topic.

188. P. 73b, s.v. *hiluchach*.

the physical world on Shabbos as well, for he has a balanced approach to this world. It is an unfortunate reality that many who grow inspired and are newly observant can make this mistake, in their truly righteously fueled passion, of pushing too quickly. If you see a friend making what appear to be radical changes, even for the good, see this as a call for help—for there is likely a big collapse coming. It is very important to be happy with one's level of observance and trajectory of growth, for succumbing to impatience, no matter how well intentioned, can be devastating.

But that is not the only reason that one needs to have a deep sense of happiness in his spiritual achievement. There is another very profound reason.

Money, Money, Money!

"One who loves money will never have enough money," said King Solomon.[189] Our Sages added,[190] "One who loves mitzvos will never have enough mitzvos." One who has one hundred coins wants two hundred.[191] If one loves money, one will never

---

189. *Koheles* 5:9.
190. *Vayikra Rabbah* 22:2, cited by Rashi to *Koheles, ad loc.*
191. *Koheles Rabbah* 1:34, 3:12. The actual expression so famous among *sefarim* of "*yesh lo maneh, rotzeh masayim*" is not found exactly in the words of our Sages, though the above Midrashim do say it in other words. See *Meat Tzari* of R. Yosef Tzvi Halperin-Halpert (Jerusalem 5739, 21b), where he makes this point. See also *Alfa Beisa Tinyaisa de-Shmuel Ziera*, Vol. 1, pp. 381–2. (Note also the comment of *Nefesh Yehudah* to *Menoras ha-Maor* (Abohav) *Ner ha-Rishon*, where on the statement, "No man dies with even half of his desires realized," he comments (emphasis added), "If one has one hundred, he wants *another* two hundred." It seems that he understood this expression to

be satisfied with his money. No matter how much he has and how much joy he gets from it, this will not deter him from making his next dollar. In fact, the opposite is true. When one really loves making money, he will find even more motivation to earn more and more. The same is true about our spiritual achievements. When a person really feels good about the mitzvah that he does, he will then never get enough of the mitzvos, for he will have motivation to grow even more. Though somewhat counterintuitive, the very best way to motivate someone to do more is by making them feel just wonderful about the little bit that they are presently accomplishing. One who feels that his achievements are not worth much will not expect great things on his next attempt. But the sweeter the taste of the Torah and mitzvah, the more likely it will be that one will achieve more, and even more.

---

mean that one who has one hundred wants to have three hundred, and thus he explained that one never even has half of what he is seeking, since he wants to make double what he already has, in addition to what he has already. The *Meat Tzari* tells a story of the saintly R. Zvi Hirsch of Ziditchov, who was once staying at a very wealthy man's home, and in the room where he was staying were many valuables. When the homeowner came into the room at one point, he noticed the Ziditchover lost in thought, standing above the silver cabinet. Noticing the man's surprise at catching him apparently so intrigued with the valuables, he explained that he had always wondered: Since a person has the one hundred and wants the two hundred, how can our Sages then say that a person doesn't have *even* half of what he desired when he dies? He does have the half! He explained that since people keep their silver in mirrored cabinets, it really looks like they have double! And they want to double that which they see, so really, a person is always trying to quadruple what he presently has, and so he never can die with even half of what he desires, only a quarter.

We need to feel absolutely outstanding about whatever Torah observances we are getting right, for those feelings are beyond precious. The thrill for making money, and the passion that drives people to stay up nights and leave behind comforts of home to risk life and limb crossing deserts[192] to seek their fortunes is a parallel desire to the passion for Torah and mitzvos. King Solomon wrote[193] about Torah wisdom, "If you will seek it as one does silver, and you will search for it as one does a buried treasure, you will then understand the awe of Hashem and find knowledge of God." One can only, it seems, understand what the awe of God is like, and achieve true knowledge of Him if one can tap into the passion for growth that one finds in the financial fortune seekers of the world. To love what we accomplish religiously is such a precious thing. It can bring a person to the highest of heights, and these feelings needs to be nurtured, teach our sages.

Closeness

A critical part of the *teshuvah* process is feeling close to Hashem, and feeling that we are spiritually connected. *Hashivenu Hashem elecha ve-nashuvah,* says the familiar verse in *Eichah*,[194] which means, "Return us to you, Hashem, and then we will return." It almost sounds meaningless at first glance; what can one return

---

192. See Rambam's introduction to *Perush ha-Mishnayos*: "If not for these crazy people [who travel to distant places to make money], the world would be desolate!" We benefit a great deal from the hard work of these people to keep our supermarkets and department stores well stocked.
193. *Mishlei* 2:4–5.
194. 5:21.

to if one has already been returned? If an owner finds his lost dog and returns home with him, is there any more returning to do? What this verse means is that once we discover that no matter how far we journeyed, we were always close to Hashem, then we can do the important work of returning the rest of the way. If we do not learn that we are, indeed, close, we can make the mistake of throwing in the towel. So we ask Hashem to bring us close to Him. Once we feel good about our spiritual achievements, we can truly begin the push forward to really do proper *teshuvah* and fashion the relationship with Hashem that we ought to have.

King David looked back on his great accomplishment of having complete confidence in Hashem and belief in Him. He knew that had he not had the sort of trust in Hashem that he did, he wouldn't have had the wonderful results that he did. Elul, the month of repairing mistakes and charting a new path, must also be a month of deep appreciation for achievements of the past. Elul is, after all, the same letters as *lulei*. Knowing what we have done in the past, and valuing it, is a great key to future success. King David knew this—and he wanted us all to know it too.

14

Kavei

קַוֵּה אֶל ה׳ חֲזַק וְיַאֲמֵץ לִבֶּךָ וְקַוֵּה אֶל ה׳:

Hope to Hashem, strengthen yourself and He will give
you courage, and hope to Hashem.

One is expected to be of strength and courage. If a person is
fearful, he is considered a sinner, teaches the *Gemara*.[195] Since
it is Hashem Who is in control of what happens in this world,
fearing anything or anyone is, at its root, connected to sin,
for in some way, it presupposes that Hashem is absent. This is
certainly a lofty level, not something that we achieve overnight,
but rather bit by bit, over the course of a lifetime.

R. Moshe Alshich explains that there is a potential pitfall for
someone who experiences security and confidence at the exalted
level expected of us, as described in this piece of *Tehillim*.[196] For,

195. *Brachos* 60a, based on *Yeshaya* 33:14.
196. *Romemos El* to *Tehillim* 27 (p. 112 in Wagschall edition).

when a person does not fear when facing an army, as expressed in verse 3, this could lead to conceit. It could bring a person to falsely conclude that he is the one who is powerful. Feelings of extreme confidence can breed recklessness. Caution is always prudent. Who would want to be a passenger in a car whose driver felt he was too good to exude any caution at all?

The Alshich explains that this is the message of our verse. Hope to Hashem. And when you find that your heart is confident, and strong, do not cease trusting fully in Hashem, for you will lose that protection while reveling in your self-glorification; instead, continue to hope to Hashem.

Don't Be So Confident

The principle here is that a person must be aware that his greatness is not his own strength. One's *yetzer hara* is simply too strong to beat on one's own, teaches the *Gemara*,[197] and only Hashem's help can save a person from succumbing to his desires. If this is so, then doing our part must essentially be committing ourselves to Hashem. That is the hard part and it is when we do so that we have succeeded.

The arrogance of "I know I can handle that," is a dangerous feeling. Rambam lets us know that disregard for *yichud* (the prohibitions on men and women who aren't married to one another, or closely related, being alone together in certain situations) is the primary cause of people committing adulterous

---

197. *Sukkah* 52b.

sin.[198] What he is teaching us is that even the most committed and well-intentioned people are nevertheless weak. He describes how the great Rabbis of the Talmud would warn their students, "Don't leave me alone with a woman" to teach them that there is nothing to be embarrassed about in admitting weakness. The mark of greatness is not the absence of temptation or weakness. It is the knowledge of how to turn to Hashem and avoid pitfalls. Avoiding entering the room is the primary way to succeed—entering confidently, thinking, "I can handle this," is generally foolhardy.

Wisdom from Rome

When Rabbi Yehudah HaNasi, compiler of the Mishnah, and Marcus Aurelius Antoninus would speak, they would discuss Torah ideas together. They once spoke about whether the *yetzer hara* is present in a baby while developing in the womb.[199] Antoninus said, "No. If it were present in a fetus, he would kick his way out of his mother's womb, and leave!" The *yetzer hara*, then, is the part of your psyche that pushes you to believe that you are more developed than you actually are. It is the part of us that relishes challenge, rather than ducking from it. If a fetus were to have that thought process in the womb, it would manifest itself in the fetus, wishing to jump out of the womb when vital organs are not yet ready, and that child would simply not survive.

---

198. *Issurei Biah* 22:20.
199. *Sanhedrin* 91b. For a more detailed treatment of this passage, see the chapter on *Bereshis* in my book, *Paradise: Breathtaking Strolls Through the Length and Breadth of Torah.*

The academies of Hillel and Shammai intensely debated[200] the issue of whether or not life was to be seen as good for a person, or not.[201] Would we be better off if we had never been born, and never offered the chance to achieve? On the one hand, we'd miss the greatest of opportunities. But on the other hand, we would never sin and could lose nothing either. This debate raged for quite some time, until they agreed that "it would have been better for man not to have been created, than to have been created, but now that he is alive, let him carefully examine his deeds." This is not an abstract question by any means; it is a very practical one. We learn that one is meant to engage the world with caution, knowing that there is a great deal of danger lurking. We are to realize that there is such potential to ruin our connection to Hashem in this life, and this concern is meant to propel us into making careful choices. Just as a man who loves his wife dearly wishes that he would never even be tempted toward being unfaithful, so should a human orient himself toward Hashem. "If only there were not even a choice of temptation. But now that I am here, I will be very careful." Though we were created to withstand challenge, we still ask Hashem daily in our morning blessings that He not bring us to challenges, for the chief weapon in our arsenal that can bring us success is our genuine fear of challenge, because of our passion for Hashem and for doing what is right.

---

200. *Eruvin* 13b.

201. See Vilna Gaon to *Iyov*, where he discusses how, certainly, life must be good if it is a gift from God, and understands this *Gemara* to be speaking about reincarnation.

Rosh Hashanah: The Anniversary of Sin

Rosh Hashanah was the day that man was created,[202] and thus was the day of Adam's sin. It is a day when mankind entered a world of challenge. Before the sin, Adam and Chava were pure and untainted; temptation was not present in the way it was after the sin.[203] They walked around unclothed[204] and didn't know shame or lust. Before Adam and Chava ate from the forbidden fruit, evil was a reality that was external to their bodies. In practical terms, this means that the desires of their bodies were in confluence with the desires of their souls. Their physical bodies actually desired to be healthy, to grow, to accomplish, and to spiritually transcend. Conflict between soul and body didn't exist before the sin. After eating from the tree, things radically changed. [205] Adam and Chava chose to eat from the tree. They chose to enter a world of challenge.

Rosh Hashanah is our day to justify man's creation; we celebrate it.[206] Paradoxically, we celebrate it by acknowledging its risks, and being aware of the Day of Justice, which reminds us that there are consequences to our deeds. The key to great success is

202. *Pirkei de-Rabbi Eliezer* 8; see explanation of Maharsha to *Rosh Hashanah* 27b, to explain why we call this Hashem's first day of creation. See also the important words of *Pri Tzaddik*, on *Rosh Hashanah* 6, who elaborates on the connection between Rosh Hashanah and the *Gemara* in *Eruvin* cited above.
203. Rashi to *Bereshis* 2:25.
204. *Bereshis* 2:25.
205. *Nefesh ha-Chaim, shaar* 1, Chap. 6. For a thorough treatment of this subject, see R. Chaim Friedlander, *Sifsei Chaim, Emunah u-Bechirah*, Vol. 2, p. 107.
206. For more on this, see R. Dovid Cohen's *Massas Kappai* Vol. 3, p. 101, s.v. *Shacharis ba-shofar*.

here in this last verse of *Le-Dovid*. Hope to Hashem, and when you succeed, remain humble and grateful; don't be cocky. Just turn around once more and hope to Hashem.

Other Works by
Rabbi Elchanan Shoff

El Mikomo Shoaif, Jerusalem 2008

Va-Ani Bahashem Atzapeh on *Tehillim,* Jerusalem 2010

Melo Chaf Nachas: 20 Approaches to One Fantastic Agaddah,
Jerusalem 2012

Birchasa ve-Shirasa on *Maseches Brachos,* Jerusalem 2012

*Paradise: Breathtaking Strolls Through The Length and Breadth
of Torah,* Jerusalem 2012

Eilecha Eschanan on *Tehillim,* Los Angeles 2015

9 781947 857094